LIVING
the SAVVY *life*

The Savvy Woman's Guide to
Smart Spending and Rich Living

MELISSA TOSETTI AND KEVIN GIBBONS

NEW YORK

LIVING *the* SAVVY *life*

The Savvy Woman's Guide to Smart Spending and Rich Living

MELISSA TOSETTI AND KEVIN GIBBONS

© 2011 Melissa Tosetti and Kevin Gibbons. All rights reserved.

ISBN 978-160037-834-8 (paperback)

Library of Congress Control Number: 2010932581

Published by:

MORGAN JAMES PUBLISHING
The Entrepreneurial Publisher
5 Penn Plaza, 23rd Floor
New York City, New York 10001
(212) 655-5470 Office
(516) 908-4496 Fax
www.MorganJamesPublishing.com

Cover Design by:
Rachel Lopez
Rachel@r2cdesign.com

Interior Design by:
Bonnie Bushman
bbushman@bresnan.net

In an effort to support local communities, raise awareness and funds, Morgan James Publishing donates one percent of all book sales for the life of each book to Habitat for Humanity.
Get involved today, visit
www.HelpHabitatForHumanity.org.

Acknowledgments

We would like to thank everyone who allowed us to share their stories. You are the inspiration behind a movement toward a life of savvy living.

We would also like to thank Carla Ada, Cheryl Broadway, Renee Hardiman, Linda Haze, Erika Lawrence, Laura Lentz, Sue Widup and Gary Smith for their keen editing eyes, attention to detail, feedback, inspiration and support.

We want to thank Chefs Mark Parker and Jennifer Whitmire-Parker for joining us in our quest to help people become more comfortable in the kitchen.

From Melissa

I want to thank my mom and dad for instilling in me the belief that I can do anything I set my mind to and encouraging me to follow my writing path.

I want to thank my grandmother for all of the savvy lessons she taught me.

I want to thank Jimmy Haze for being such a cool and encouraging brother.

I want to thank Paul and Joan Tosetti for their continuous support.

I want to thank my husband Paul for his tolerance and steadfast support as we worked to figure out and define this savvy life, together.

I want to thank my son Dante for inspiring me to work a little harder while writing this book, so we have even more time together in the immediate future.

From Kevin

I would like to thank my parents Alice and George for teaching me how to save money and the value of waiting for things.

Thank you to my friend and first boss, Virgle Hedgecoth, who taught me how to spend money and enjoy the good things in life without guilt.

Thank you to my wife, Leta, who is continuously teaching me that the most valuable things in life aren't things and are beyond price.

Table of Contents

Money Affects Everything

I find it romantic to believe that money isn't important. How wonderful would it be to live life without being burdened by monetary details? But the truth is, money affects every aspect of our lives. It affects how we dress, where we live, what we eat and how we spend our free time. It affects our emotions and enhances or detracts from our enjoyment of life.

There are an abundance of good personal finance books and resources out there offering tips on everything from cutting coupons to investing in your 401(k). However, effective money management is about so much more than retirement plans and saving money at the grocery store. To illustrate this point, we offer you a brief comparison of the lives of an Average Woman and a Savvy Woman:

An Average Woman

An Average Woman has no idea how much money is in her checking account at any given time. She often uses her debit card with a knot in her stomach, hoping it will not be declined.

She has a closet overflowing with clothes, few of which can be pulled together into a complete outfit. Many of the clothes in her closet still have the tags on them because she realized she has nothing to wear with the item once she brought it home. She continues to purchase clothes at random, always feeling the need to buy more.

She finds herself in the drive-thru several days a week because her kitchen cupboards are bare. When she does buy groceries, she does so without a plan and isn't quite sure what to do with them once she gets home. When she goes to her favorite high-end restaurants, she feels a tinge of guilt as she pulls out her credit card to pay the bill.

She takes a vacation at least once a year with several weekend getaways interspersed. She finds herself preoccupied while on holiday since she was just on the verge of paying off her previous vacation when she headed out the door.

An Average Woman is a consumer who keeps buying, hoping the next item she purchases will magically create the life she so desperately wants.

A Savvy Woman

A Savvy Woman knows exactly how much money she has in the bank and always spends less than she makes. Her growing savings account gives her a confidence that is visible to others.

She has a pared down wardrobe comprised only of clothes she loves, look great on her and make her feel good. She is a style setter, not a trend follower. Because she knows what looks good on her, she can shop at discount stores and look like she shops at high-end boutiques. She is willing to invest in her wardrobe, but asks if an item will be going on sale. She shops with purpose, yet she is open to serendipitous moments. She never purchases an item for her wardrobe unless she has fallen in love with it.

She cooks the majority of her meals at home. She has numerous dishes mastered and is always on the lookout for new recipes to add to her repertoire. She has a black belt in grocery shopping, and her pantry and refrigerator are stocked full of ingredients ready to be made into delicious meals. The fact that she cooks the majority of her meals at home allows her to enjoy the occasional meal out at her favorite high-end restaurant, without guilt to spoil the experience.

She has an appetite for adventure and consciously saves money for those long weekends away and the trip to Italy she has been planning for the past year. When she vacations, the trip is paid for prior to departure, so it is a true holiday.

A Savvy Woman picks and chooses what she brings into her life, being selective versus mindlessly consuming. This control over her financial life allows for even greater *joie de vivre*.

Does the Average Woman's life sound a little familiar? Are there times when your paycheck doesn't last until the next payday? Is your closet overflowing with clothes, but you have nothing to wear? Do you have trouble fully enjoying a vacation or dinner out knowing that you put it on your credit card? Perhaps there are certain aspects of your life that you have under control, but you get derailed by holidays, special occasions or when your car unexpectedly breaks down.

The Impact

Of course, not having control of your financial life puts understandable stress on you, but how does it affect those around you?

Do you and your spouse argue about money or silly things that ultimately relate back to money? If you have children, are they aware of your anxiety? As they look forward to a special occasion, do they know you dread not knowing how you are going to pay for it?

Does your concern over money affect your relationship with your friends? Do you agree to go out to meals or other social events knowing that you "can't afford it" or that you would rather be spending your money on something else? Do you then resent your friends for putting this strain on your life?

If you relate to any of the situations above, it may be overwhelming to think about what it would take to transform your life from that of an

Average Woman to a Savvy Woman. Before you lose hope, think about what it is costing you physically, emotionally and financially to continue on your current path. Now, take a few minutes and think of what you could achieve by making that transformation. Is it the thought of a closet full of wearable clothes that gets you excited? How about a vacation with your friends that is paid for in advance? How wonderful would it feel to put together a memorable holiday for your family without ever touching a credit card? Would you love to pay cash for a romantic dinner at your favorite restaurant with your significant other?

It isn't about how much money you make. No matter how much or how little money you earn, the key to financial success is to spend less than you make. Unfortunately, the majority of Americans spend without thought, wasting money on purchases that give them little satisfaction for their investment. You often see this careless spending in the form of clutter. Learning how to focus your spending on what is truly important to you and economizing on those things that are not as important to you is key to a savvy life.

It's not only spending less than you make and focusing your spending, but it's also getting and staying organized that is crucial to achieving and maintaining a savvy life.

Melissa's Transformation

In 1994 at the age of 24, I moved to the San Francisco Bay Area to be with Paul, my then boyfriend, now husband. When I moved, I had a decent amount of debt and was in sticker-shock at the astronomical price of rent. What I would have paid for my own apartment in Fresno, CA barely paid the rent for a room in someone else's home. I began working in a public relations firm as a receptionist by day and I waited tables at night. I managed to pay off my debt in a year and happily quit waitressing, dropping down to a much more manageable 40 hour work week.

Although my debt was now paid, I still didn't have much money to play with at the end of each paycheck. Through trial and error, I became more disciplined in my money habits. I also started to look for ways to get creative in how I spent my discretionary income. I began reading everything I could get my hands on about frugality. By this time, the Internet was coming into its own and I became an avid reader of *The Dollar Stretcher* website. I devoured *The Tightwad Gazette* books by Amy Dacyczyn and became inspired by Tracy McBride's *Frugal Luxuries* books. From these and countless other resources, I applied as many of the suggestions as I could. Paul was very tolerant as I continuously experimented with ways to save money. I started to think about what I could do with less. How could I make what I had stretch further? How many different ways could I wear that one piece of clothing?

I also began to study the habits of everyone around me. I was mesmerized by my coworker Jessica who had a natural talent for finding the coolest clothes at thrift stores. I was impressed by my friend Leta whose home was decorated with bargains she found at antique stores. I followed the adventures of my friend Sophie, who had a knack for finding concert tickets and vacation deals for next to nothing. I loved visiting my in-laws who entertained effortlessly, putting delicious, yet inexpensive meals on the table. I was fascinated by my friends Gina and Kathleen who could shop at Target and look like they just walked out of Nordstrom.

I watched these wonderful, budget savvy people around me as I took notes and asked questions. How did you refinish that table? Where did you buy that beautiful bracelet? How did you make that mouthwatering roast?

I studied the women of World War II who, during a time of sacrifice and rationing, became fashion icons with their red lips and perfect hair. I loved reading about the tricks they came up with like drawing lines on the back of their bare legs to give the illusion of wearing stockings.

As I became a master in frugality, I did my best to suppress the desire to go to nice restaurants for dinner or to museums and the theater. What I couldn't control was my passionate desire to travel. I began to wonder if frugality had to be an all-or-nothing commitment. Did frugality have to be an unconditional way of life or was there another way? I started to realize that if I focused my frugal talents on the things that weren't as important to me, then I could focus spending on the things that were important to me.

Very soon, we were able to reap the benefit of this philosophy. We started with a goal of a seven day trip to Disney World. Over the course of a year, we looked for every way possible to save money for that trip. By the time we boarded the plane, the trip was paid for and we were able to spend as we pleased in the land of The Mouse. Our spending included an unforgettable six-course dinner and wine pairing at Victoria & Albert's restaurant at Disney World's Grand Floridian Resort.

That trip was a powerful lesson to us. By focusing our spending, we could have and do the things we truly wanted. The idea of saving on the things that are not as important to us so we could afford to spend money on the things that are important to us became a way of life.

What You Will Find In This Book

As you will see throughout this book, financial management isn't always about buying an item on sale or shoveling money into your savings account. It's about taking care of what you have so it lasts as long as possible. It's about managing your kitchen properly to ensure you don't throw money away in the form of leftovers or spoiled vegetables. It's about regularly wearing 80% of the clothes you own instead of 20% and leaving the rest to hang like dollar signs relegated to the back of the closet. It's about proper skin care now so you don't have to spend big bucks on skin repair items later.

Together, we will create a lifestyle that includes all the things you desire. We will do this through managing your finances, focusing your spending, taking inventory of what you already have and taking care of what you already own. First, we start by adopting the Savvy Life Philosophy and following the Golden Rule, which you will learn about in Chapters 1 and 2. From there, you will learn the six habits that allow you to put the Savvy Life Philosophy in place. Once that ground work is set, we get to have fun! We will look at each area of your life including:

- your home
- vacations, hobbies, entertaining and dining out
- clothes and accessories
- skin care, cosmetics and hair care
- cooking and kitchen management
- savvy money management

At first glance, it may not seem that the amount of clothes in your closet has anything to do with your vacations or what you eat for dinner. Actually, it's all related. You have a set amount of money that comes in each month to allocate to the various areas of your life, such as paying bills, buying groceries, shopping for clothes and setting aside money for your next vacation. How you manage each of those areas of your life directly impacts the others.

Throughout this book, I will introduce you to friends and readers of The Savvy Life (www.thesavvylife.com), the online magazine we have published for the past five years. You will read their stories, see the lessons they taught us and how they transformed their own lives.

Although *Living the Savvy Life* is filled with ways to save money, it isn't about frugal living. It's about finding and maintaining balance. Americans are extreme junkies. We love extreme reality television shows like *The Biggest Loser* where contestants go from overeating as a way of life to the strictest of dieting and exercise regimens. The thought of simply eating less and exercising more is not as interesting to us as watching someone endure wacky fitness and nutrition challenges.

This extremist behavior occurs with our money as well. During economic crises, we swing from a lifelong habit of overspending to extreme frugality. We vow to never dine out again and to pour every penny into savings. What typically occurs is we stick to it for a week, maybe a month. Then, like binging on ice cream after a crash diet, we go on a spending spree, often spending more than we would have prior to our vow of frugality.

Hey, I love a good challenge, but when it comes to long lasting results, extreme is rarely the solution. Lasting lifestyle changes are most successfully achieved in baby steps. It's time we all step off the pendulum that swings between overspending and extreme frugality.

Is This Book for You?

In the Savvy Living courses I teach throughout the San Francisco Bay Area, I was initially startled to see that the typical class had an average age of 60 and was comprised of many women making six-figure salaries. With retirement just a few years away and a potential reduction in their monthly income looming, they realized they needed to do something about their money management habits, and fast.

As you will hear us emphasize again and again, it doesn't matter how much money you make. It's how much you keep! The debt Michael Jackson left behind and the financial devastation photographer Annie Liebovitz experienced are both perfect examples of that rule.

While *Living the Savvy Life* is written for women, the lessons within are directly relevant to men, teenagers and families. Although you could consider this a personal finance book, it is intended as a lifestyle primer. The advice given is a little bit mom, dad, grandma, grandpa, financial advisor, best friend, that favorite wealthy uncle and that ever-stylish aunt.

What do we want you to get out of this book? We want you to gain control of your finances, focus your spending on what you truly want and enjoy your life to the fullest! We want you to stop worrying about your credit card bills or how you are going to make it to the next paycheck. Life is a wonderful adventure, regardless of how much money you are making. Together we can create a plan to finance it properly.

Chapter 1

The Savvy Life
Philosophy

Shortly after I moved to the San Francisco Bay Area, Paul and I joined a kung fu school. It wasn't long before martial arts became a big part of our lives. Paul, a natural athlete, was immediately noticed by the Master of the school and within less than a year, he was asked to become a full time instructor for its San Mateo, CA location. Within two years, he was promoted to head instructor. I continued my own training achieving first a black belt, then first degree and then second degree. Little did we know when we started that our martial arts path would mirror our savvy life path.

In 2006, Paul decided it was time to move on, and the following year we opened Fearless Fitness Martial Arts Training and Development Center in Foster City, CA. The aspect of martial arts Paul and I most enjoyed was sparring. So we decided to focus on teaching a mixture of striking, grappling and takedowns. Our timing was serendipitous. Two months after we opened, The Ultimate Fighter reality television show premiered. The show revived the Ultimate Fighting Championship (UFC) promotion company and turned mixed martial arts (MMA) into the fastest growing sport in the world.

Although sparring was our primary focus, we also wanted to teach the training techniques for MMA without students having to actually fight or make physical contact. I teamed up with one of our coaches, Erika Lawrence, and together we created the FFIT (Fearless Fitness Intensity Training) program. We like to describe it as MMA based and influenced by yoga, Pilates, bootcamp and second grade recess.

As Erika and I worked with our students, we listened to their previous weight loss struggles and heard the same diet-and-gain, diet-and-gain patterns. We knew that without creating lifestyle changes, those destructive patterns would continue. We designed a nutrition program focusing on portion control and consuming whole foods. However, recognizing the importance of food in our culture and quality of life, we figured out ways for students to still enjoy the foods they love so much, but in moderation.

From the inception of The Savvy Life website, I wrote about the similarity between controlling spending and controlling weight. As I continued working with students at Fearless Fitness, those similarities became glaring. I recognized that it didn't matter if I was standing in front of a class at Chabot College in Hayward, CA teaching money management or if I was doing a consultation with a Fearless Fitness student, the message was the same: focus your calories and focus your money on the things that are truly important to you.

With calories, it's about enjoying a mouthwatering, fresh-out-of-the-oven homemade cookie instead of wasting calories on a processed pre-packaged cookie that you find in the vending machine at work.

With money, it's about focusing your spending on the new jacket you really want versus impulse buying trendy tops you won't wear in six months because they've gone out of style.

It's all about making your dollar count and spending it on the things that give you pleasure versus mindlessly spending. The Savvy Life Philosophy and overall theme of this book is:

Save money on the things that aren't as important to you so you can afford to spend money on the things that are important to you.

It sounds easy, right? And yet, how many times have you gone into a store such as Target or Wal-Mart for one or two items and walked back to your car pushing a shopping cart loaded with bags? As you walked through the store, things kept "jumping" into your cart. You didn't realize how many stowaways you had until you started loading your car.

Before you beat yourself up, don't feel bad. Stores spend millions of dollars on psychological studies, advertising and marketing to persuade you to impulse buy. Once you identify the trend of random items jumping into your cart, it is very easy to steel yourself and focus your spending on the items you actually walked into the store to purchase - the items that are genuinely important to you.

The Savvy Life Philosophy in Action

The Savvy Life Philosophy works on a small scale such as the store, but it also works on a grand scale.

A more substantial example of the Savvy Life Philosophy is the way Paul and I look at cars and travel. Paul and I are passionate about travel. Our trips are very important to us. What we aren't passionate about are cars. They are simply a way for us to get from point A to point B. Because cars are merely tools for us, we purchase reliable used cars rather than spending over $30k for brand new vehicles. The money we save by not having two separate $400-$500 car payments allows us to spend on what is important to us: travel. That philosophy has taken us beyond our initial trip to Disney World. Three of our favorite adventures so far include:

- A week exploring the castles and history of Scotland and Orkney.
- A tour of China where we climbed The Great Wall and trained with the Shaolin Monks.
- A 10 day Alaskan cruise with our, then 2 year old, son Dante.

The Savvy Life Philosophy is really that simple. First, we identified what is important to us - travel. Then we identified what isn't important to us - new cars. We figured out a way to save money on cars and focused our dollar on what is important to us - travel.

Travel is also important to co-author and Savvy Life's Managing Editor Kevin and his wife Leta, but they enjoy doing it on their motorcycles. One of their favorite things to do is head out on their bikes for an extended trip. They will camp two or three nights and then splurge one night at a very nice inn. They save up for these trips by identifying and saving on something that isn't important to them - cable TV which can exceed $100 monthly. Instead, they save that $100 per month for their motorcycle trips.

One of my favorite examples of the Savvy Life Philosophy in action was put into practice by my friend Erin. I met Erin through Fearless Fitness. She moved to the San Francisco Bay Area from Vancouver, Canada and works as a nurse. A few months after joining Fearless, Erin's boyfriend Steve asked her to marry him. The engaged couple decided that purchasing a house was their number one priority and started looking for ways to save money. Erin had attended one of our Savvy Life seminars and asked to pick my brain about their finances and goal.

Erin is a naturally savvy woman and I was impressed with how well she managed her money. We identified a few additional areas to tighten up her spending, but it was Erin who chose a way to make the biggest impact on their savings. She decided to move into Steve's tiny apartment prior to their wedding so they could immediately start saving more than half of what they were separately spending on rent.

Erin identified what is important to her - owning her own home. She also identified what isn't as important to her - living in her own large apartment. At the time of this writing, she and Steve are happily married and are very close to having enough money for the down payment of their first home.

Everyone's passions and interests are different which is why the Savvy Life Philosophy is just that - a philosophy. It is up to you to decide how to apply it to your life. In Chapter 12, you will have a chance to review a series of questions that will help you put the Savvy Life Philosophy into action.

Chapter 2

The Golden Rule

How many times have you told yourself: "If I just made a little more money, I would be OK."

It is easy and understandable to assume that if we just made a little more money it would solve our financial problems. However, it's typical for us to increase our spending with each raise, never giving ourselves the opportunity to catch up. If you increase your spending with every raise, it doesn't matter how much money you make. In fact, if this is your habit, the more money you make, the more dangerous your situation becomes. Your debt load gets bigger and bigger, to the point that it becomes impossible to get out.

In this chapter, we will look at:

- The Golden Rule
- The harm of overspending
- Successful role models
- Why we overspend
- The intangible benefits of following the Golden Rule

There are dozens of financial software products on the market and hundreds of books that have been written about managing personal finance - all of which have their benefits. However, like many things in life, the solution for successfully managing your finances is simple. The only way to achieve financial success and the Golden Rule of finance is:

Spend less than you make.

That's it. It doesn't matter how much you invest or how well your 401(k) is doing. If you spend more than you make, you will always be financially at risk.

Over the years of publishing articles on savvy living, we have come across people who make $115,000 annually, but spend $127,000. They have little, if any, savings and no comprehension of where their money goes despite their six figure salary. We have also met people who make $45,000 annually and spend just $36,000. They diligently put money in their 401(k) and have a healthy, growing savings account.

Spending less than you make sounds easy enough, right? And yet, according to a February 15, 2009 article on *Forbes.com*, "Eight Reasons Why We Overspend," the average American spends $1.33 for every $1.00 they make. With a $50,000 income, they spend $66,500 that same year. That is $16,500 more than they earn. If this habit continues, that $16,500 of debt turns into $33,000 the following year, $49,500 the next year and so on. None of these figures factor in the devastating cost of compounding interest.

Those who find themselves in this cycle have no opportunity for savings and no opportunity for security. All of their discretionary income becomes and remains focused on paying off their ever-mounting debt.

Overspending on a Small Scale

I once worked in a very difficult office environment. One of my colleagues was the executive assistant to the CEO. Her job was brutal and emotionally taxing. Every morning she came in and sucked it up because it was the only job at the time that would allow her to maintain her lifestyle. She drove a Mercedes she was making payments on, had a $1,000 a month clothing habit, and her hair easily cost $200 every six weeks to maintain. There were many things she could have done to reduce her cost of living such as scale back or reduce her clothes shopping. She had plenty of clothes to "shop her closet" for several years. Instead, she found herself trapped by spending more than she made. She further compounded her situation by increasing her spending with every raise rather than using the extra money to reduce her debt.

Overspending on a Grand Scale

Occasionally, I will hear someone say, "He has so much money, he couldn't spend it all." That statement makes me cringe. Celebrities, professional athletes and lottery winners continually make headlines with their poor financial habits. Michael Jackson is the poster child for how not to handle your finances.

According to a June 26, 2009 article in *Time Magazine* titled "What Happened to Michael Jackson's Millions?" Jackson pocketed more than $300 million from sales of his recordings since the early 1980s. In 1985 he purchased the rights to a catalog of music that included 251 Beatles songs. Those rights, as well as concerts, endorsements and music videos, would generate more than $400 million over the next two decades. And yet, in 2003 it was reported that Jackson regularly spent $20 - $30 million more each year than he earned. It is estimated that upon Jackson's death, he was $300 - 400 million in debt.

Another case of spending more than you earn on a grand scale is that of famed photographer Annie Leibovitz. Despite a seven figure salary from *Vanity Fair* and earning tens of thousands of dollars per day from celebrity clients such as Louis Vuitton, in 2009 Leibovitz found herself in default of a $24 million loan. Her debtors threatened to take two of her homes and worse, seize control of her entire photography collection.

Who is Doing it Right?

On the opposite end of the spectrum, famed investor Warren Buffett prefers a modest life. He still lives in the same Omaha, Nebraska home he purchased for just $31,500 more than 50 years ago. He drove a 2001 Lincoln Town Car for years which he bought second hand. Buffett had a net worth in excess of $37 billion in 2009 and yet lives off an annual salary of $100,000. That's just 0.00027%! Talk about spending less than you make!

Jay Leno is another great example of a wealthy individual doing it right. In a September 6, 2009 interview with *Parade* magazine he said, "When I was a kid, I had two jobs. I worked at a Ford dealership and at a McDonald's. I'd spend the money from one job and save the money from the other. That's still the way I am now. I live on the money I make as a comedian, and I put all the TV money in the bank. I've never spent a dime of TV money - ever."

In addition to following the Golden Rule of spending less than he makes, Leno embodies the Savvy Life Philosophy when it comes to his passion for collecting cars and motorcycles. His smart day-to-day money habits allow him the ability to joyfully focus on his passion for all things automotive.

Why Do We Spend More Than We Make?

One of the biggest reasons we overspend is the ability to get credit so easily. Walk onto any college campus in the United States during the first week of school and you will see companies lined up offering free gifts for signing up for a credit card. Head to the cash register of many major retailers and they will offer you an immediate discount if you open a store credit card.

One effect of this phenomenon is the fact that Americans carry an average of $8,700 in credit card debt. In 2008, the median annual household income was $52,029. That means the average American is in debt by over 16.5% of their income and that doesn't include mortgage and car payment debt.

Another reason we overspend is we bank on that next paycheck. Expecting another paycheck in a few days or a week gives a false sense of security that money is unlimited. The problem with this habit is we continuously find ourselves in debt to the following paycheck and never give ourselves the opportunity to catch up.

One of the most sobering lessons of the 2008 recession is that paychecks are not guaranteed. In that year, 1.2 million people lost their jobs. Spending into the following paycheck is the first habit to break.

The Perks

In addition to a growing savings account, the benefits of spending less than you make are tremendous. If you are unhappy in your job situation, it is easier to leave for a new position, even if it means taking a reduction in salary. As the economy ebbs and flows you will not feel as subject to its whims.

The psychological impact of debt and overspending is devastating. It causes feelings of anxiety, embarrassment and fear. Spending less than you make gives you control over your finances which, in turn, positively affects your emotional well being. It inspires wonderful feelings of confidence and control giving you the emotional freedom to enjoy life so much more.

Breaking the cycle of overspending is achievable. By creating a few simple habits and routines, you will easily shift from spending more than you make to gaining and maintaining control of your finances. In the next chapter, we will introduce six Savvy Habits and show you just how easy it is to spend less than you make.

Chapter 3

Savvy Habits

One of the reasons so many struggle financially is a lack of education. Most people don't learn about money in school or from their parents. The good news is you can choose to educate yourself. Just by reading this book, you have made the first step towards taking control of your money instead of allowing it to control you.

Successfully managing your day-to-day finances is simply a matter of creating and sticking to fiscally healthy habits and routines. With habits and routines, handling your money becomes effortless. There are six key Savvy Habits at the core of *Living the Savvy Life*. These habits are easy to start, easy to maintain and they work.

Savvy Habit #1
Pay Yourself First

Just about every personal finance guru agrees that paying yourself first is the number one tool for successful financial management. It is also the habit that makes it easy to follow the Golden Rule and spend less than you make.

Paying yourself first is the process of making sure you consciously save for your future (both long-term and short-term), before spending on anything else, including your bills. The easiest way to do this is to have money electronically taken out of your paycheck and put into a retirement program such as a 401(k) and an emergency savings account. This process automates your way to financial success. The best part of this habit is once you initially set it up and reach your ultimate savings percentage goal, you just sit back and watch your money grow.

If you don't pay yourself first there is always something that money can be spent on instead of saving it. By automating your savings, you make the process both painless and effortless.

How Much Should You Save?

Financial advisors typically recommend a savings goal of 15% of your income. It's the maximum amount you can set aside in most retirement programs. This money is for your retirement. The objective is to set it aside, untouched and let it grow.

But, what about that emergency savings account you're supposed to have? Over the early part of the 21st century, the recommended size of this fund has grown from three month's salary to as much as one year's salary. How much you to set aside should be based on your personal situation. At minimum, your emergency account should have enough money in it to cover three months of living expenses. Beyond that, it is up to you.

We saw a wonderful quote years ago that has always stuck with us.

"Save 20% and spend the rest with abandon."

Doesn't that sound wonderful? How would it impact you emotionally to know that you are systematically saving 20% of your income and that it is growing exponentially with each paycheck?

We believe that 20% is a solid savings goal. Fifteen percent of that savings is for your retirement and 5% is for your emergency savings account. Once that emergency fund has been established, you can start concentrating on saving that money in a separate account for a home, to replace your car or whatever your needs may be.

How on Earth Can I Save 20%?

If you are struggling to save anything right now, that 20% will feel like an overwhelming number. The good news is that we don't expect you to start saving that much right away.

Even if you could buckle down and start putting away that much money now, it's likely you will do great for a week, maybe a month, but at some point - like a crash diet - you will break down. Instead of binge eating a double cheeseburger, large fries and a soda, you will likely go on a spending binge. You will then think you are weak-willed, which you aren't, and get too frustrated to want to save anything at all.

Instead, we suggest that you make small goals. As suggested by Robert Kiyosaki, the author of *Rich Dad Poor Dad*, start by being an underachiever. Begin with a small goal that you know you will be able to attain. For example, if you really want to start saving an extra $50 per paycheck:

- Start by saving $25 for a few paychecks.

- Next, try saving $35 for a few more paychecks.

- Once you achieve those first two goals, saving $50 a month will be easy.

Remember, only save what you know you can save. If you are pulling money from your savings account on a regular basis, you're not saving. If you find that you are dipping into your account, cut back the amount you are saving by a few dollars and when you are ready, you can increase the amount again.

Retirement or Savings First?

What is most important, your retirement or emergency savings account? Understandably, there is confusion as to what account to focus on first. The answer is both. It is imperative to start putting money away for your future immediately. It is just as urgent to start putting money away for an emergency.

Your 401(k) is for you to enjoy a comfortable retirement and without immediately putting money into it, that retirement might not be as comfortable as you would like. At the same time, your emergency account is there for unexpected crises and might need to be implemented at any time. If you are focusing all of your money on your retirement, the likelihood of having to use your credit cards for an emergency goes up, which will immediately put you in debt. Focus on both accounts at the same time.

If your company offers to match up to a certain amount you put into your 401(k), do your best to put in at least that amount to start. Otherwise, you are not taking full advantage of your salary and leaving money on the table. There are two things to remember about retirement savings accounts like 401(k)s or IRAs:

1. The money you put away is tax-deferred, so it is an even greater savings.

2. It is never too early to start putting money in a retirement account. Due to the nature of compound interest, the bulk of your earnings come from your earliest deposits.

At the same time, begin your emergency savings account. Even if you can only put $5 into that account each paycheck, you are at least starting to practice the habit of saving.

Want to get to that 20% goal faster?

The next time you get a raise, put the entire amount toward your savings accounts. Don't be tempted to increase your spending. You know that you can successfully live off of the money you earned prior to the raise. Pretend as though you never received it and put the entire amount into your 401(k) and emergency account. It is an effortless way to achieve your savings goal. Consider breaking down your raise so that 75% of the money goes into your retirement savings and 25% goes into your emergency savings. (The actual breakdown will depend on your personal financial situation.)

If you get a 5% yearly raise, and you put all of that money into savings, it will take just 4 years until you are saving 20% of your initial salary.

Example: Starting salary $10,000

Year	5% of Salary	New Salary	Savings	% of Original Salary	% of New Salary
1	$500	$10,500	$500	5%	4.8%
2	$525	$11,025	$1,025	10.3%	9.3%
3	$551	$11,576	$1,576	15.8%	13.6%
4	$579	$12,155	$2,155	21.6%	17.7%
5	$608	$12,763	$2,763	27.6%	21.6%

In five years, your salary will have increased from $10,000 to $12,763. If you put all that increase into savings, you will be saving $2,763, which is over 20% of your new salary.

Start Now!

If you do not already have a retirement account set up, start now! Immediately contact your human resources department and get the paperwork you need to sign up. You can put as little as 1% or even just $25 per paycheck in most 401(k)'s, so do it! If you don't have access to a 401(k) program, you can sign up for an IRA.

If you are self employed you have a variety of retirement account options. Contact an investment advisor to set up an account that best suits your needs. If you don't have an investment advisor, ask your family, friends, or your tax advisor if they have any recommendations.

Next, if you don't already have an emergency account set up, contact your bank and open one. If you are worried about that money being too easy to access, create an account at a different bank or an online bank such as ING Direct. With ING Direct, you can open an account with as little as $5.

Note: Your emergency savings account should be separate from any other savings account you may have. If you combine accounts, it can be too tempting to "borrow" from your emergency fund for other expenditures. Worse, you may accidentally dip into it with devastating consequences.

Set a deadline for creating each of these accounts. Promise yourself to start both before your next paycheck. If you need even more incentive, tell yourself that you cannot spend a dime of that next paycheck until both of these accounts have been created.

Be the Turtle

When it comes to achieving your savings goals, slow down and take it in baby steps. Even if it takes you a few months to achieve your initial savings goals, that is a small amount of time based on how many paychecks you will receive over the course of your career. Don't worry about trying to do it all at once. Initially, creating and sticking to your savings habit is the most important part of the process. Even if your preliminary savings are minimal, it is better to save something than nothing at all.

Be the turtle, not the hare. To use the diet analogy again, crash diets don't work - you need a lifestyle change. A commitment to slowly and steadily achieving your goals is easy and more likely to be successful.

Savvy Habit #2
Track Your Spending

Have you ever logged into your bank account to check your balance and panicked when you realized you had spent more than you thought? Savvy Habit #2 is the process of tracking your spending and the one that keeps you from accidentally overspending.

I have met very few people who can keep a running total of their expenditures in their head. I easily forget that I bought a second bag of dog food for $20 because it was on sale and that I put an extra $40 of gas in my car after driving to visit my family over the weekend, thus leaving me $60 less than I was expecting to have in my account. If I don't track my spending on a daily basis, I am almost guaranteed to overspend.

To track my spending, I use a simple Excel spreadsheet that is set up similar to the register the bank sends you along with your blank checks.

#	Date	Transaction	Withdrawal	Deposit	Balance	x
	2/15	Salary		1,000.00	1,000.00	x
239	2/15	Safeway Grocery	-75.00		925.00	x

Each morning, I open the spreadsheet and enter my spending for the previous day. I then log into my bank account and check what expenses have cleared marking an "x" next to those items. This second step helps me ensure that I don't get surprised by anything such as an online purchase I made or an automatic withdrawal I may have forgotten about.

If I am not careful and I allow other things to get in the way of this habit, it becomes very easy to overspend. Another reason I like to do this on a daily basis is because if I stay on top of it, it takes just a few minutes each day to do. If I wait a few days, it takes longer to catch up. Then my instinct to procrastinate kicks in, turning it into a chore.

Until he got in this practice, my husband Paul would get nailed by online expenditures. It would happen most often when he would order a book from Amazon that was backordered. It is Amazon's practice to not charge your account until your book has shipped. Paul would then forget about it until a month later when he would check his online balance and there would be a lot less money then he expected. He would then see that Amazon had shipped his book, debiting his account at the same time. It wasn't until he started tracking his spending that he was able to stop this cycle.

In Chapter 11 (ironically labeled) we will go into greater detail about different ways to track your spending from something as simple as that check register to various financial software packages.

Savvy Habit #3
Pay All of Your Bills on Payday

Of all the Savvy Habits, this is one of my favorites. There is something empowering about it that makes me feel in control of my spending and of my time. Savvy Habit #3 is to pay all of your bills on payday before spending a penny of your paycheck on anything else. You have already automated your savings so you have taken care of paying yourself first. Now you can turn your focus to paying your bills.

The benefits of paying your bills on payday include:

- Ensures the money to pay your bills is available.

- Eliminates late fees, which is one of the greatest wastes of money.

- Strengthens your credit score.

- Gives you peace of mind, knowing that your bills have been paid.

Paying all of your bills on payday is another example of how habits and routines make managing your finances effortless. The first few times you sit down to implement this habit it may feel a little overwhelming. Once you get the hang of it, you will actually look forward to the process and enjoy that feeling of control.

Making it a ritual will help keep the process simple and enjoyable.

- Before payday, ensure that all of your bills are in one place.

- Make sure you have been staying on top of Savvy Habit #2 and always keep track of your spending. You don't want any surprises when you sit down to pay your bills.

- Try to pay your bills first thing in the morning with as little distraction as possible. The later in the day you do it, the easier it is to push off until the following day.

Food and Gas

Over the course of the current pay period the two things you are most likely to need are food and gas. In addition to paying your bills on payday, it is also the best time to fill your car with gas and to purchase your groceries. By making both of these purchases on payday or, as close to payday as possible, you are ensuring these crucial items are available to you.

In Chapter 10 we will go over simple ways to plan your meals and create grocery lists, so don't feel overwhelmed right now at the thought of doing your grocery shopping. One more note regarding the grocery store: if you like to withdraw a certain amount of cash each pay period, consider withdrawing it when you get your groceries. Most stores allow you to get cash with your grocery purchase without charging a fee. Doing so will save you additional time and gas by not having to make an extra trip to the bank.

The bonus of purchasing your groceries and gas on payday is that in one day you take care of three of your biggest weekly (or bi-weekly) chores and procure the items that are most crucial. Also, now that your bills have been paid, your gas tank is full and you have plenty of groceries in your kitchen, you know exactly how much discretionary income you have for that pay period to spend. How great will it feel knowing that you have taken care of all of the important responsibilities and that the money you have left over is yours to spend as you please?

Finally, on payday, check your calendar for upcoming one-time expenses, like birthdays, anniversaries or planned trips. Later in the book, we talk about how to plan for these expenses, but making a quick double-check part of this habit will save you from last minute surprises.

Savvy Habit #4
Set Financial Goals

The fact that you are reading this book about personal finance means you probably have a desire to purchase a big ticket item at some point in the future. Is it a new house, a car or a dream vacation? Perhaps you really want to focus on achieving the security of having three to six month's salary set aside in your emergency savings account. Whatever your desire, the process of setting a goal will help you focus and attain what you want far faster than simply wishing for it. It is much easier to realize your dreams once they are clearly defined.

I am a big goal setter and believe this is one of the key habits that helped Paul and me achieve the things that are important to us such as travel, starting our businesses and remodeling our home.

Throughout this book we will discuss setting goals and offer suggestions to focus on and achieve them. To give you an example, let's start with the goal of accumulating enough money for a down payment on a house.

It would be easy to decide that you need money for a down payment. It is likely that within a certain amount of time you will achieve that goal. However, there are ways to be far more proactive about achieving that goal.

To start, do a little research on the neighborhood you want to live in and the price of homes in that area. If possible, visit open houses to give yourself a solid idea of what the houses in that price range look and feel like.

If you find one or two houses that fit into your dream, take photos of them. Although it is likely those particular houses won't be available when you are ready to buy, you will have a visual reminder of your ultimate goal.

Next, find out exactly how much money you would need to put down for a house in that price range. Talk to a real estate agent about the realistic costs of how much you need to purchase your home including closing costs, taxes, insurance, etc. Once you have that number, write it down and keep it.

If you don't already have a savings account dedicated to this goal, open one. This account is separate from your emergency savings - although once you have reached your emergency savings goal, you can dedicate the monthly amount you were saving for that to your house account.

Now, give yourself visual reminders of your goal. This will help keep you on track. Post photos of that house on your refrigerator and next to your computer. Most importantly, place a small photo of your house inside of your wallet. Every time you go to pull out your debit or credit card to spend on something that isn't as important to you, you will have a visual reminder of what is most important to you - your house. You can even go a step further and put a sticky note titled "My House" on your debit and credit cards. Each time you want to use your cards you will be reminded and motivated again to save for that house.

Finally, decide on a realistic date when you want to achieve your goal. Be careful not to say, "In two years I want to buy my house." It is very easy for "two years" to always be two years from today. Instead, decide that, "By April 30, 20__ I will put the down payment on my new home." Even if you miss the exact date, you will be far closer to your goal than if you didn't set a date at all. And who knows, you may be able to reach that goal far faster than you anticipated!

Finally, by setting goals, each time you have a windfall it will be easy for you to put that money into your goal account rather than to come up with some other way to spend it. Stay focused.

Savvy Habit #5
Know When to Invest and When to Bargain Shop

In the last 40 years, ours has become a disposable society. The availability of cheap, throw away items is ubiquitous. It is very easy to automatically reach for the less expensive item. However, routinely purchasing the cheaper item can cost you more in the long run.

Before making a purchase, think about what you need it for and how long you want it to last. Then decide if it's time to invest or bargain shop. Making the decision to invest or bargain shop takes place whether you are talking about a piece of clothing or a dishwasher.

In the case of an article of clothing, if you decide to purchase a new sweater you have two choices. You can easily go to a disposable fashion store such as Forever 21 and invest $19 on a sweater. Typically, with disposable fashion, money is saved by making the garments as fast as possible and the attention to detail in finishing stitches is not always there. It is possible that your $19 investment will last just one season. If during that one season you wore that sweater 12 times, the cost per wear would be $1.58.

If you go to a higher end store and choose to spend an additional $10 looking for a sweater in the $29 range, the attention to detail is most likely greater and that sweater could last you five years or more. If during that five year time period you wore the sweater 100 times, the cost per wear would be $.29.

In Chapter 13, Savvy Shopping, we offer more detail about investing versus bargain shopping.

Savvy Habit #6
Spend Money on the Things You Want

Savvy Habit #6 is the practice of focusing your spending on the things you want. It falls right in-line with the Savvy Life Philosophy of saving money on the things that aren't as important to you so you can afford to spend money on the things that are most important to you.

When shopping or just going about our day, it is very easy for us to get distracted from the things we truly want. Remember, advertisers spend millions on research and studies to figure out how to create campaigns that will make us part with our money. Just knowing that makes it much easier to stay focused.

This habit is best practiced as you approach the check out register. No matter what type of store you are in, take a quick survey of the items you have and make sure they are the things you intended on purchasing in the first place and that you really want. If any stowaways jumped into your hands, turn around and put them back. Stay focused and only spend money on the things you really want.

In Chapter 13, we also go into greater detail about the habit of spending money on the things you want and include plenty of tools and fun ideas for keeping you focused.

Take Your Time

New habits take time to master, so don't give up. Studies show that it takes 30-45 days for an activity to become a habit. With a little trial and time, the habits will become routine and second nature.

Chapter 4

You Can
Afford It

<u>STOP!</u> Stop saying you "can't afford it." The fact is that - you can.

- If you made more money, you could.
- If you didn't have a car payment, you could.
- If your mortgage was lower, you could.

There may be caveats, but you can afford anything! Being able to afford what you want is about choices. Whether that choice involves doing something to make more money or lowering your cost of living:

- You chose to work in a career earning your current salary.
- You chose to buy the car you drive.
- You chose to live in your current home.

The point is that you are in charge of your money. Money in and money out - you make the decisions.

There isn't an invisible sign placed on your head at birth limiting the amount of money you can make or how to spend it. We have within our power the ability to change our circumstances whether that is making more money or spending less.

In this chapter, we will look at:

- How to improve your current salary.

- How to increase your income.

- How to refocus your spending.

- How to change your thinking about money.

Your Current Salary

I understand there may be circumstances for why you are staying in the job you currently have. Perhaps you are a single parent and it allows you to be there when your children come home from school. Perhaps it is the highest paying job you can find with your current skill set. We often feel trapped by these circumstances and are too deep in the trenches to see the opportunities that are around us. The good news is that those opportunities are out there.

While working as an office manager, I had the pleasure of meeting Cesar who was the building's janitor. Cesar often brought in new pictures to show me of his two boys. One day I saw him in the break room poring over a book. I asked him what he was reading and he told me that he was going to night school to study computer science. Here was a guy who was willing to put in the time to get the skills necessary for a better paying job. He had to temporarily sacrifice a few hours a week with his family to make it happen, but at the same time, he was teaching his sons the lesson that we all have control over our future.

Another way to make more money is to ask for it. Carla A. is one of my savviest friends and is very shrewd when it comes to her salary. Prior to each review, she makes a long list of her accomplishments since her previous review and all of the benefits she personally brings to the company. She then asks for a raise and even gives her boss a specific number. This habit of taking control has afforded Carla a steady and significant increase in salary over the years.

In her book, *Women, Work & the Art of Savoir Faire: Business Sense & Sensibility*, Mireille Guiliano went through a similar practice each time she was up for review at champagne maker Veuve Clicquot. "I always went into my own salary reviews with a carefully reasoned benchmark range for what I thought I was worth to the company."

No one says you have to stay in the job you currently hold. If you aren't that thrilled with where you work, start looking for a new job. Again, go into the interview with a number. The important thing is to ask for the salary you want. Don't leave it up to them and hope they offer the salary you desire.

There are More Than 40 Hours in a Week

Another option is to get a second job. Who says you have to restrict working to just 40 hours a week? Get a second job associated with a hobby you love. Make it a job you will really enjoy so it won't seem like work.

My friend Jannette approached me a few years ago asking for advice. Through credit cards, car and student loans, she found herself over $100,000 in debt and was overwhelmed and hopeless. She didn't know what to do. We started by sitting down and organizing her finances so she could see everything very clearly. Next, we devised a plan that allowed her to pay all of her bills as well as set aside a small amount in an emergency and retirement account. The process of getting organized and creating a plan made her feel in control and empowered. She decided that she wanted to do more.

A nurse by trade, Jannette asked around and found a second nursing job that she could do in addition to her current one. She then went from having just $100 extra per month outside of necessary expenses to over $1,500 extra per month. She has buckled down and is aggressively paying off her debt and increasing her savings. At the same time, she still has enough money left over to have some fun. Jannette is a perfect example of someone who took control and I always tell her story in our seminars.

Another one of my favorite stories of someone who did what it takes is told in Jack Canfield's book, *The Success Principles*. He tells the story of Debbie Macomber who dreamed of becoming a writer, despite being dyslexic and only having a high school education. Each morning, this stay at home mom would pull out her rented typewriter after her four kids went to school and start working. When her husband and children came home, she would move the typewriter off the kitchen table and make dinner. When the kids went to bed she would drag the typewriter out again and continue working. This went on for 2 ½ years.

One night, her husband Wayne told her that money was getting too tight and if they were going to survive she needed to get a job. Realizing how difficult it already was to find enough time for her book, she knew she couldn't work a full time job and finish it at the same time. Wanting the best for her family, she laid awake trying to let go of her dream. Sensing her despair, her husband asked what was wrong and she explained how much she believed she could make it as a writer. Wayne's response was, "All right, honey, go for it." As a family, they buckled down and saved as much money as possible: forgoing vacations, pinching pennies and wearing second hand clothes for another 2 ½ years.

Debbie and her family's sacrifice and persistence paid off. In 1984, her book *Heartsong* was published. Since then, she has gone on to write over 150 books. Her husband Wayne was able to retire at the age of 50 and spends his time building an airplane in the basement of their 7,000 square foot mansion. Debbie and Wayne also taught their children the very important lesson that with focus and hard work you can make your dreams come true.

In Chapter 2, I discussed my former colleague who stayed in a job that made her miserable because she wasn't willing to lower her standard of living. That was a choice she made. It was more important for her to drive a Mercedes and spend $1,000 on clothes every month than to be happy at work.

In contrast, my friend Sue has what she calls a "Time to Go" account. Having completed her emergency fund years ago, she started this account for the times when she realizes she doesn't enjoy her job anymore. Her "Time to Go" fund allows her to quit her job when she wants to instead of having to wait until she finds a new one.

Shift Your Spending

Is your car payment killing you financially? Are you not in love with that car anymore? If you can do it without taking a loss, sell it! Sell your car and invest the money in a reliable used car. No one says you have to own the particular car you have.

The same goes with your house. Whether you rent or own, no one says you have to live in a particular sized house in a particular neighborhood. This is much easier done if you are renting, however, if you own, consider your options for downsizing and talk it over with a financial expert to see if it is a good decision for you.

My friend Sally purchased a house in November 2008 as a fixer-upper. She admits to being naïve about the full financial picture this placed her in and didn't take into account taxes, higher utility bills and a devastating plumbing issue. By May 2009, she was "robbing Peter to pay Paul."

Unfortunately, this was at the height of the recession and she felt trapped. Instead of panicking, she made a plan, starting with cutting back on all non-necessary expenditures and staying on top of her bills as best as she could. She put sweat equity into the house and placed it on the market eight months after she bought it. Because of the work she put into the house, she was able to sell it and actually make a profit. Sally was smart enough to recognize immediately that she was in over her head and took action! In fact, that action earned her an extra $80,000 in a terrible economy allowing her to pay off all of her bills and walk away from the situation debt free and wiser for the experience.

My friend Carla S., mother of two beautiful little girls, worked full time. When her kids reached the ages of three and four, she decided that she wanted to spend more time with them and started thinking about converting to part time work. She and her husband were always savvy with their money, maxing out their 401(k) contributions and systematically putting money into their emergency savings account; but they knew there were other ways to save. She came to me and asked for my advice on lowering her grocery bill and other ways to spend less. With just a few tweaks, they were able to adjust their expenditures and Carla began working part time without having to make any major sacrifices. The extra time also gave Carla the opportunity to trade working three hours a week at her yoga studio in exchange for free unlimited yoga. This time-for-yoga exchange has saved Carla $180 per month.

The examples above are of people that either found themselves in an uncomfortable financial situation or decided they wanted more and did something about it. Some of these ideas may sound extreme and take you out of your comfort zone. The ideas sound extreme because your neighbors (the Joneses) aren't doing it. That's a good thing. Mimicking the Joneses is a dangerous habit. Besides, wouldn't you rather blaze your own trail than follow theirs? If you are truly unhappy with your financial situation and want more, be willing to do what it takes. Be willing to work for what you want and get creative!

Notice we are not saying that you deserve all the money you desire, or that all you have to do is wish and it will come true. In every example we have shown you, the people have worked for what they wanted. What we are saying is that you are in control of your life and you make the choices that will give you success. It may take time and work, but you can change your situation.

Money and Attitude

Your attitude about money makes an enormous impact on your financial happiness and success. It's OK to want a new house. It's OK to want a new car. It's OK to want a wardrobe full of clothes that look great on you. It's OK to want to travel the world. What is not OK is to complain about what you don't have. Complaining is a waste of energy. It's draining on you and those around you. Instead of complaining, focus on setting goals so you can attain what you want. As we have said above, you can afford anything. It's just a matter of doing what it takes to achieve those goals.

Everything in life is about choices and control. If you really want something, make that a priority in your life and devise a plan to accomplish it. If you try for something, you actually have a pretty good chance of getting it. If you don't try for it, you are almost guaranteed to not get it.

As you work toward your goals, the process of taking action will give you that first taste of taking and having control. As you start to achieve your smaller goals, you will realize your bigger goals are within your reach.

The one pitfall of setting goals is that they can make you blind to the joys of the present. A former colleague of mine had a personality quirk that, once I recognized it, broke my heart. No matter what she bought or achieved, she was never satisfied or happy. She wasn't necessarily an impulse buyer. If something she wanted was out of her price range, she wouldn't buy it. Having bailed herself out of debt twice before, she was very good about saving for what she wanted. But in the meantime, she would obsess over it. That item would consume her and would be all that she could think or talk about until she could finally purchase it. Sadly, she would be happy for a day or two and then something else would catch her eye and she would fall back into the pattern of obsessing. It was as if she didn't have the ability to relax and enjoy what she already owned.

She taught me the very important lesson that there is a balance between striving for goals and being content with what you already have. Focus only on your goals and it's difficult to appreciate where you are today. Be complacent with what you already have and it's difficult to find the momentum to move toward your goals. In that balance is happiness and fulfillment.

Appreciation

A key component to living the savvy life is to appreciate and take care of what you already have. If your goal is to purchase a new car and in the meantime you're driving an old car, keep it clean and ensure it receives proper maintenance. Taking care of what you already have will help you better enjoy the time it takes to achieve your goal. Also, it will help make your initial investment (that old car) last as long as possible.

The same goes for your house. You may not love where you are living, but keeping your home clean and well maintained will help you like it a little more while you work toward your goal of a new home.

Taking care of what you have applies to all things in your life - your clothes, appliances, computer, gadgets and furniture. Take care of and appreciate what you already have and set goals to achieve your desires. While it is important to dream, don't fall into the trap of living for tomorrow. Do what you can to appreciate today.

Chapter 5

Where We Spend Our Money

As outlined at the beginning of this book, money affects all areas of our lives. We spend it to eat and provide shelter. We spend it to put clothes on our back and for entertainment. When we spend or save in one particular area, it affects how much we have left to spend in other areas. An example of this interdependence happens when you call for pizza delivery the night you think you are too tired to cook. That call directly affects the amount of money you will have left for that upcoming weekend getaway you have planned.

The next six chapters are broken down into different areas of our lives that are most impacted by our finances. In addition to being filled with money saving ideas, each chapter will help you think about your own life and where you want to focus your spending and where you want to save.

Chapter 6 - Home

Your home should be a place of refuge, a haven. It should be where you are the most comfortable. From cleaning and maintenance to decorating, this chapter introduces ways to affordably create a personal sanctuary that is a reflection of you.

Chapter 7 - Entertainment

Rest and relaxation are necessities of life. Enjoy your time off from work even more by being financially smart about your activities. This chapter introduces ways to save on travel, entertainment and having fun. Discover what you really consider recreation and relaxation, and how to achieve that joy on a reasonable budget.

Chapter 8 - Wardrobe

This chapter focuses on creating a wardrobe filled only with clothes that make you look and feel wonderful. The goal of this section is for you to be able to wear 80% of what is in your closet on a regular basis rather than the typical 20%. In this chapter you will learn how to shop for your own body and how to purchase clothes you will actually wear, getting very picky about what you bring home.

Chapter 9 - Beauty

It's very easy to go broke on skin care, hair care and cosmetics. This chapter includes information from interviews with makeup artists and hairstylists offering money saving tips and ideas.

Chapter 10 - Food

Cooking your own meals is one of the most impactful ways to save money. Food is an integral part of our traditions, culture and celebration. Meals should be savored and ritualized, not endured in the name of frugality. This chapter focuses on cooking and kitchen management basics to help you enjoy delicious food and save money while providing a nourishing experience.

Chapter 11 - Money

The amount of information available on personal finance is overwhelming. In Chapter 3, we touched on the six habits and routines that are the solution to managing your finances successfully. This chapter concentrates on the other aspects of personal finance that will be the greatest contribution to your fiscal success, such as getting and keeping your finances organized, different ways to pay down debt and the power of anticipation.

The next six chapters are where the Savvy Life Philosophy really comes into play. We all have different priorities, and our priorities can change throughout our lives. As we review each area think about your own life and what is most important to you, so you can focus your spending there. Then identify where you can save money on the areas that aren't important to you.

Keep in mind that this isn't an all-or-nothing process. You don't have to be dedicated to a certain area of your life such as your wardrobe. If clothes are important to you, that doesn't mean you have to spend every last penny on them. That would put you out of balance. However, if clothes are important to you, it is likely that you will want to focus more of your money and attention on your wardrobe and perhaps food is where you would work harder to save money.

Are you ready? This is the fun part!

Chapter 6

Home

In this chapter, we will look at:

- The devastating effect of clutter.
- Establishing your own simple cleaning routine.
- How to build a Home Management Notebook.
- Creating a home that is reflective of your personality.
- Taking care of what you already own.

Melissa's Story

For many years, I couldn't relax in my own home. It was so cluttered that I always felt on edge. Each room was a visual reminder of all the cleaning and organizing that I needed to do - cleaning and organizing that was never finished. I continuously felt my energy being drained away and my stress and exhaustion intensify. I would get so frustrated that the only time I felt relaxed was while on vacation staying in a hotel. I kept thinking, "Shouldn't I be able to relax in my own home?"

In the back of my mind, I knew the clutter was also an indication that I didn't have my financial house in order. Yes, I was paying my bills on time and staying debt free, but I wasn't managing my money once it transitioned from cash to a possession. I would go shopping for clothes and what I would purchase would stay in the bags on the couch for a week. If I really wanted those items, they would have been taken out of the bags and hung on hangers as soon as I got home. The clutter would not let me find the black shoe polish I needed so I would have to buy another bottle. Inevitably, the next day I would find not only the original bottle of shoe polish, but the two other bottles I had purchased the last time I couldn't find the original bottle.

It sounds dramatic, but I would literally panic any time someone would knock on the door. Paul's mom was one of the most organized, neatest women I had ever met. Several times she caught me at home with my house in embarrassing order. I found myself constantly apologizing to my friends for the state of our house. After a while, I couldn't fake that it was a temporary situation.

When Paul and I would entertain, I would do marathon cleaning sessions prior to the party. By the time our guests arrived, I would be exhausted and a tiny bit grouchy. I knew there had to be a better way.

The sad part about the situation is that I actually enjoy housecleaning. Growing up on a few acres in Fresno, my chores included your basic sweeping, mopping and vacuuming. I read each issue of *Martha Stewart Living* from cover to cover and my bookshelves were filled with books on home keeping such as *Mrs. Beeton's Book of Household Management.* I knew how to clean the house, I just couldn't stay on top of the cleaning and get it uncluttered and organized.

I finally hit a breaking point and decided to take a few days off from work to focus on the problem. The week before my grand makeover, I was psyched and excited about the clean up. I even cleared my schedule the evening before that first vacation day so I could jump right in. I likened my cleanup project to the makeover shows that were becoming so popular. I knew it was going to be hard work, but by the end of the weekend, my house was going to be magically transformed into a Zen-like retreat.

When I got home from work that day I changed clothes, pushed up my sleeves and immediately -- became overwhelmed and started crying. I didn't know where to begin. Within 30 minutes I made the excuse that I needed plastic bins to organize my stuff and left the house. I didn't come back until after 9:00 pm, because I couldn't face it. I ended up spending a silly amount of money bringing more stuff into my home - the plastic bins. Ultimately, I wasted my vacation days, accomplished nothing and my depression grew. The following Monday I found the Flylady.

Marla Cilley, a.k.a., the Flylady, is the founder of the Flylady.net website. She offers advice on how to organize your home and ultimately, your life. She breaks the decluttering and cleaning process down into small, manageable steps, which is in direct contrast to my "get it all done in one long weekend" tactic. No wonder I became overwhelmed.

As I started following her decluttering process, I began to feel an ownership of my home that I had never felt before. As the clutter left, I started to feel control over our house. An almost immediate result of this process is that I became very conscious of what I brought home. I started to get extremely selective about what I purchased; only picking up items that I fell in love with and that reflected my personality. I had been unconscious of how much money I was spending on random stuff for the house. A surprising byproduct was the immediate positive impact on our finances for being so selective.

Clutter Free is Key

As you can see from my own personal experience, clutter is expensive as well as physically and emotionally draining. Clutter hides the items you have already purchased, so you have to purchase them again. Clutter forces you to purchase organizing bins so you have a place to put it - so you can buy even more clutter. It's a vicious cycle.

Clutter can make you think you need a bigger house. Moving is expensive and bigger homes mean bigger mortgages. Clutter, like a goldfish, will grow to the size of its environment. How soon before you think you need an even bigger house?

Clutter makes us rent storage facilities. The problem with storage facilities is that you only think about what is inside of them once a month when you pay the bill. After moving out of a house and into an apartment, my friend Gary paid $210 every month for five years to store his stuff. When he finally moved back into a house and went to get his stuff he decided to go through his items before bringing them home. Of everything he had stored, he only brought home one filing cabinet of business papers and two boxes of photos. The rest, he no longer wanted. Ultimately, Gary paid $12,600 to store the file cabinet, photos and what he deemed as clutter.

You have the power to conquer clutter. Whether you choose to follow the Flylady system or tackle it on your own, you can do it. Take it one stack, one box, one drawer at a time. With a steady, systematic approach, your house will be clutter free.

Keeping it Clean

Investing in artwork, painting your walls and buying new furniture won't make a positive visual impact if your house isn't clean. Coming home each day to a clean home will give you a sense of serenity, allowing you to enjoy that freshly painted wall, new artwork or piece of furniture so much more.

Keeping a clean home also helps save you money. When the kitchen is clean and there are no dirty dishes in the sink, it's much more inviting to cook. When your home is clean, it's much more relaxing to be home so the desire to go out, and ultimately spend additional money, isn't as strong.

I believe my own struggle with keeping my house clean is similar to others. Although we understand the mechanics of sweeping and mopping, it's the lack of a routine that gets us into trouble. If my floors were just a little dirty, I wouldn't worry about mopping them. It was almost as if they had to become a biological hazard before they would get my attention. By then, the rest of the house would also be at that state so I would become overwhelmed.

Once the clutter was removed, the process of creating and implementing a cleaning routine really gave me control over my house. The key was to manage small amounts of dirt before they became large ones. The Flylady's website is a wonderful resource for creating such routines, but there are many others. Type "housekeeping" into the search tool on Amazon.com and you will see over 4,000 results. Like managing your finances, successfully managing your home is a matter of creating habits and routines.

As I mentioned in Chapter 3, Savvy Habits, I can't keep a mental running total of how much money I have in my checking account. My brain just doesn't work that way. I have to keep track of everything on paper. I also have a difficult time staying on top of keeping our home clean if I don't keep a list of my habits and routines. If I try to keep it all in my head, I get overwhelmed.

I created a Home Management Notebook based on the Flylady's system that I keep in my FranklinCovey™ Planner. Within the notebook, I have listed what I want to stay on top of on a daily basis, on a weekly basis and on a monthly basis. Instead of having to think about what needs to get done, I just look at my list and start working.

Daily Habits

- Put dishes directly into dishwasher.
- Immediately clean up after ourselves.
- Take out garbage and recycling as needed.
- Focus on one project at a time.
- Melissa will do 10 - 15 minutes of housework each morning.
- Paul will do the majority of the laundry and at least one other chore a day.
- Dante will clean up his toys every evening.

Weekly Cleaning List

- Monday - Sweep and mop
- Tuesday - Garbage to curb
- Wednesday - Clean dog's dishes

- Thursday - Dust and vacuum
- Friday - Clean bathroom
- Weekend - Launder bed linen

Monthly Habits Broken Down Week by Week

Week 1
Front Porch, Living and Dining Room

Front Porch
- Sweep porch
- Wipe down porch light
- Wipe down mailbox
- Clear cobwebs

Living Room
- Straighten bookcases
- Wipe knickknacks
- Clean out magazine stacks
- Clean under cushions
- Clear cobwebs
- Polish furniture
- Wipe fingerprints from walls and light faceplates
- Clean windows and sills
- Dust baseboards

Dining Room
- Dust dining set
- Clean phone
- Clear cobwebs
- Polish furniture
- Wipe fingerprints from walls and light faceplates
- Clean windows and sills
- Dust baseboards

Week 2
Kitchen and Laundry Room

Kitchen
- Empty fridge and clean thoroughly inside and out
- Clean microwave inside and out
- Clean stove and oven
- Straighten drawers and cupboards – declutter as necessary
- Scrub down cabinet and dishwasher fronts
- Clean under sink
- Clear cobwebs
- Wipe fingerprints from walls and light faceplates
- Clean windows and sills
- Dust baseboards

Laundry Room
- Wipe down the top and sides of washer and dryer
- Sweep and dust behind appliances
- Clear cobwebs
- Wipe fingerprints from walls and light faceplates
- Clean windows and sills
- Dust baseboards

Week 3
Bathroom and Dante's Room

Bathroom
- Deep clean bathtub
- Wash shower curtain
- Clean out medicine drawer
- Clean mirror
- Wipe down scale
- Run Dante's bath toys through the dishwasher
- Clear cobwebs
- Wipe fingerprints from walls and light faceplates

- Clean windows and sills
- Dust baseboards

Dante's Room
- Straighten drawers and closet
- Flip mattress
- Straighten and declutter toys
- Clean under the bed
- Straighten closet
- Donate out-grown clothes
- Clear cobwebs
- Polish furniture
- Wipe fingerprints from walls and light faceplates
- Clean windows and sills
- Dust baseboards

Week 4
The Master Bedroom and Office

Our Room
- Wash bed skirt
- Straighten shelves
- Clean under the bed
- Straighten closet
- Straighten the top shelves
- Clear cobwebs
- Polish furniture
- Wipe fingerprints from walls and light faceplates
- Clean windows and sills
- Dust baseboards

Office
- Clear off surface of desk
- Straighten one drawer at a time
- Clean the monitor screen
- Clear cobwebs

- Polish furniture
- Wipe fingerprints from walls and light faceplates
- Clean windows and sills
- Dust baseboards

I, of course, don't get it all accomplished every day, week or month, but even if I get to a few of the items, it keeps me on top of things. Most importantly, when I find that I have 5 or 10 minutes of spare time, I can just look at the list and pick something to do rather than try to think of what to do. The list allows me to automate the process. The more habits and routines I create, the more freedom I have with my spare time.

You can very easily create your own Home Management Notebook. Start by crafting cleaning routines that will work for your own home. You can pull ideas from the information above or visit the Flylady's website to see her complete list. Once you have personalized your own list of cleaning routines, you can add other home related items to the Notebook.

Your Home Management Notebook is an excellent place to keep a Home Projects List. This is a list of all the things you want to accomplish around your home such as tiling a bathroom, replacing air conditioner filters or installing a new porch light. The beauty of a Home Projects List is that like your Home Management Notebook, it allows you to put all of your project ideas in one place, getting them out of your head. Then you can prioritize from there.

Start by listing everything you would like to accomplish in your house over the next year. Include both the big and the small projects. From there, calculate how much each project will cost. Then figure out how much time each project will take. For the big projects you may want to break them down into smaller chunks so they don't feel so overwhelming. You can then tackle the items on your list based on three concepts - priority, cost and time available.

For example, a leaky faucet is going to be your highest priority. It's important to take care of that project first. From there, you can base your tasks on the amount of time and money you have available. If you know you're going to be home for the weekend and are hankering to do a project, take a look at your list. Figure out how much time and money you have to dedicate and then pick a project. This system of project management gives you the most impact for your time and money. It's surprising how much faster your projects get accomplished with this type of organization.

One note - Paul and I have found that if we purchase the supplies we need for a project on Friday night, our projects get done that much quicker on the weekend because we can get started first thing the following day. If, for some reason, we have to wait to go to the supply store on Saturday morning, the projects always seem to take twice as long. Whether it is perception or reality, shopping ahead is one of our favorite time-saving tools.

Other items to consider keeping in your Home Management Notebook include the warranty and contact repair information for your appliances, electronics and computer equipment. You can also keep a list of important contact numbers. If you have ever lost your cell phone, you know how important it is not to keep all of your telephone numbers online. It's good to have a hard copy of them and your Home Management Notebook is a savvy place to keep the list.

Your Home Management Notebook is very personal and you can put anything in there you think is important. The key is to keep it in a place that is visible and easily accessible to ensure you will use it.

Decorating is a Mindset

In this book we won't get into the bones of how to decorate. There are hundreds of great books and free resources on the Internet that can give you detailed information on the concepts. Instead, we'd rather talk about how to personalize your home.

What I find most common about decking your halls is that people have a fear of doing something wrong. Don't be afraid! Your home is your personal space where you have ultimate control. First of all, be willing to make mistakes. Paint a wall red. If you don't like it, you can paint over it. If you desire, be unconventional in where you place your furniture, lights, wall decorations, etc. It's your home and it should reflect you. There is no right or wrong. Be willing to pour your personality into your home. Make it your own sanctuary. I love going to homes that are a manifestation of the owner's personality.

My stepsister Charity has a natural talent for helping people decorate with the items they already own. She can identify common elements and has a way of pulling them together and displaying them in a manner that the owners didn't see before. As you declutter your home, you will have a chance to get reacquainted with what you already own. There may be decorating pieces you have that you just didn't see before. From there, you can figure out if you need to purchase something additional to pull those items together to make a complete picture. This is yet another way to inject your personality into your home. Use what you already own.

Paul and I have both worked in bookstores and we have a large collection of books. Over the years, they have often played a role in decorating our home. We have used a pile of books as a table of sorts or left a particular interesting-looking book out on display.

The clutter that previously filled the corners of our home has long been replaced with dark furniture that I picked up over the years on sale at Cost Plus World Markets, or the side board that I waited to go on sale at NapaStyle. Our love of history and our taste for martial arts is found throughout the house with art work and historical weapons on display. Anyone who knows us immediately "gets it".

Walk into Kevin's and his wife Leta's home and you will see her love of antiques as they are found throughout the home. Step into Kevin's office and the walls are lined with beautiful legal bookcases that Leta found in antique stores at bargain prices. You will also recognize immediately that Kevin has a thirst for books of all genres as they fill the bookcases and room. His books and her antiques always spark interesting conversations when new guests are invited to their home.

Our friend Janna's home is filled with artwork by her husband Karl, a professional artist, and pieces painted by her beloved grandmother. Again, you walk into her home and backyard and it's reflective of Janna.

Paint

I read articles all the time that say paint is a cheap form of decorating. That is both true and false. In order to paint a wall properly, you can't just purchase one can of paint and one paint brush. In most cases, you have to purchase a can of primer to prime the wall to get it ready to paint. Also, you need to have certain brushes for trim and certain rollers for surface. When you initially start, paint is not going to be cheap. However, once you have the tools (and you take proper care of them), those paint projects really do become cheap ways to redecorate.

Idea Books

An idea book is an effective tool for helping you create the space of your dreams. An idea book is simply a notebook that you use to keep pictures of rooms or decorating items that appeal to you. When you find pictures that draw your attention, cut them out and place them in your notebook. As you continue to add pictures, look for patterns in the photos such as color, texture or a common theme. This will give you a clearer picture of what you are attracted to, so you can begin to incorporate those elements into the design of your home. Note - you can always reserve a section of your Home Management Notebook to use as an idea book.

I have a wall in my office that is lined with wire and clips. I use it to plan articles for *The Savvy Life* and to post photos of places that we want to go on vacation. I also use it as an idea book of sorts where I post pictures of clothes and rooms from magazines that catch my attention. Recently, I went to post a new picture of a living room that I cut out of a magazine when I realized there was a common element of a 'tree branch' as an art piece in five of the seven photos I had posted. It was the branch that kept catching my attention. By posting the photos on the wall I was able to see this element and am now on the lookout for a specific tree branch to use as a decoration in my living room.

Once you have that clear picture of how you want to design your home, you can make a list of what you need to do to make it happen and add it to your Home Projects List. Then, make a list of what you need to purchase for your decorating project. Keep the list with you at all times. I have a small notebook in my purse that I use as a spending book. Whenever and wherever I go shopping, I pull out the book to see if there is anything I need to keep an eye out for. This spending book helps keep me focused on the things I truly want to purchase.

Adding with Discretion

Once your home is clean and clutter-free, and you have started your idea book, you can add your personal touches to transform it to reflect your personality and lifestyle. Before you consider making a single purchase, ask yourself, "Is this going to make me happy now and in the future?" Fall madly in love with an item. Don't be an easy date.

It's important to take the time to get what you want. A few years ago, Kevin and his wife Leta decided it was time to purchase a new bed. They found one at a "going out of business" sale. It wasn't exactly what they wanted, but it was a good deal. After they ordered it, the salesperson called to say the style that was actually available was a "little different" than the bed they saw in the store. Kevin and Leta cancelled the order. Even though the price was good, they did not want to compromise on a piece of furniture they expected to keep for 10-20 years. Four months later, they found exactly what they were looking for at an even better price.

When it comes to designing and decorating your home, don't be in a hurry to finish it. Let your house be a work in progress. Allow it to unfold over time just as your own personality evolves.

What's New Doesn't Always Have to be New

When looking for new items for your home, don't forget to look for "old" items. Antique shops, thrift stores, flea markets, even Internet trading sites can be treasure troves, if you know how to use them properly. In Kevin and Leta's house, there are exactly six furniture items that were purchased new, including the bed mentioned above. Every other piece of furniture, from the dining room set, to the coffee table, to the office furniture to the bedroom nightstands was previously owned. Even the entertainment center is a converted armoire from the 1930's.

Decorating with previously-owned furnishings has assets and liabilities. If done with an open mind and a little bit of knowledge, it can be a refreshing approach. As a general rule of thumb, if it has moving parts, like an appliance, you should only buy used if you have a specific need such as really wanting an authentic 1920's kitchen.

Advantages to decorating with "old stuff":

- You can find styles that are different from today's trends.

- You can find specific styles that interest you.

- Wood quality of older (pre-1940s) furniture is often better than contemporary furniture.

Risks of decorating with "old stuff":

- You buy everything "As Is." There are no warranties or exchanges.

- It can be difficult to judge quality and compare prices. You're relying on your own expertise to determine how good of a deal you are getting.

- You often only have a limited time to make a decision. Most items are one-of-a-kind and not normally "stocked".

Where to Shop

Where to shop for your home depends largely on your own personal style, but remember that you are likely to get better deals and find more unique items in non-traditional stores. The usual home improvement and furniture stores all have similar styles and prices.

I have long been a fan of Cost Plus World Markets. I like the quality of their furniture and I know that if I am patient, I can get what I want on sale. The accessories at Cost Plus also speak to my love of travel and the items tend to be unique.

Just like clothing, thrift stores are a great place to purchase accessories for the home. Picture frames, unusual table settings, figurines or art work can all be found to suit just about any taste. In general, larger furniture items are pretty low quality in thrift stores, but every so often, you may get lucky. If you keep in mind the idea of "repurposing" - using something for other than its original, obvious application - you can find all sorts of interesting furnishings in thrift stores.

Likewise, flea markets and swap meets are great for getting that certain specific small item, although Kevin and Leta did find a small student's desk that worked nicely after it was refinished. Be sure you carefully inspect anything you plan to buy at a flea market, and do be aware that flea markets are sometimes used to sell stolen property. No matter how tempting the price is, that is not the place to buy electronic equipment!

Estate sales are the liquidation of a household's items, usually after the owner has died, or moved to a much smaller residence. They are excellent places to make deals because there is very little overhead and the sellers would much rather sell the items immediately than have to ship or store them. However, because they are typically restricted to just one house, the selection can be limited. In most cases, the sales are managed by people other than the actual owners, so don't expect to be able to get much history on the items. Usually, terms of sale are cash-only, although sometimes these sales are run by specialty companies that can accommodate checks or credit cards.

Shopping at antique stores can be fun or intimidating. The key to successfully shopping at antique stores is the same as it is for shopping anywhere. Remember that you are in charge of your purchasing. Just because something has a high price, that does not make it valuable. The only difference between an "antique" and "just plain old stuff" is that somebody thinks the antique is valuable. You decide what something is worth to you, regardless of what the price tag says. Different antique stores carry different styles and quality of merchandise. Some are high-end establishments that only deal in original items in perfect condition, others sell professionally restored or repaired wares and some are little more than glorified junk stores. The only way to find out what kind of store it is, is to go inside!

When shopping for furnishings in an antique store, it is very important to keep in mind what the item will look like in your house. Antique stores specialize in beautiful things. But how is that 12-foot tall double armoire going to look in your bedroom? Are the ceilings in your bedroom high enough to accommodate it? Will it even fit through your front door?

You can always negotiate on price in an antique store. (You can always try to bargain in any store. The worst they can do is say "no"). Typically, a dealer will give a 10-15% discount if they want to move the item. As a common courtesy, however, only ask if you are really serious about buying. Also, most antique stores have a three-month layaway policy. They keep the item in the store while you make three equal payments over three months at no interest. This is a great way to buy bigger-ticket items, but remember that if you miss a payment, you forfeit both the item and your previous payments, so stay current.

Finally, don't overlook the benefits of the Internet. Buying small, relatively inexpensive items over the Internet is fine, but we still recommend physically seeing larger furnishings in person before you buy. Swap services, such as Craigslist and Freecycle are good sources of deals, if you know what to look for and are careful in your purchases. Kevin and his wife purchased an $1800 oven for $250 on Craigslist. What are the steps to take when making such a purchase?

- Think safety first and be aware of your surroundings. Once you arrive at the address, if you don't feel comfortable, leave. Nothing is worth risking your well being.

- Always take someone with you and let a third person know where you are going and how long you expect to be gone.

- Be aware of stories that are too good to be true. In the case of the oven, the homeowner was remodeling, replacing an electric oven with a gas one. When Kevin and Leta went to check the oven, they actually saw the replacement in the garage waiting to be installed.

- Verify that the item is the one advertised and works properly.

Bartering sites help you take advantage of great deals and are environmentally friendly as well. If you haven't investigated this source for your home needs, you may want to give it a try.

Cut Flowers versus Houseplants

Flowers and plants add a beauty and tranquility that is hard to equal. Whether you use cut flowers or living houseplants depends on your own style and how green your thumb is.

Are you the type of person that likes new color and changing décor? Do you have trouble keeping plants alive for more than a few weeks? For some, regular watering can be a challenge. Cut flowers are an easy way to add variety to your living space.

If you like the variety and color of cut flowers, shop smart. In addition to flower shops, many grocery stores carry cut flowers as well, often at good prices. Check to see if your city has a wholesale flower market. San Francisco has a very well-known Flower Mart that provides cut flowers to florists, businesses and private individuals at wholesale prices. Buy in season and avoid holiday specials. At Valentine's Day, roses easily double in price, while carnations can be found for next to nothing.

Taking care of your cut flowers will make sure you get your money's worth. Get them home and in water as soon as you can. Always cut off the bottom 1-2 inches of the stems before you put them in water. Plants have a natural damage control similar to blood clotting that causes cut ends to seal up. If you do not give the flowers a fresh cut, they cannot draw water. If the flowers come with a food packet, be sure to use it. You do not need to change the water in a cut-flower vase, but be sure to keep it full. As long as the ends are immersed in water, they won't seal up, but as soon as they are exposed to air, they will start clotting.

If you think replacing flowers every two weeks is too pricey, or you get depressed every time cut flowers start to wilt, then living houseplants are more suitable for you. Again, shop smart. Grocery stores and home improvement centers are good sources for living plants. Nurseries have a greater selection, but you pay for that specialization. Unless you are looking for something exotic, try the other places first. If you do not have much experience with houseplants, start small, with hearty plants like philodendrons, spider plants or English Ivy. Talk to experts in the nurseries (information is free) or home improvement centers to determine the best plant for your living conditions. You need to consider such things as room temperature, amount of light, traffic, pets and small children. A window-sill herb garden in your kitchen is a practical, as well as beautiful way to add plants to your home.

Take Care of What You Have

I remember when Paul and I first moved in together, neither one of us had a bathroom scale. This was at a point where I was working two jobs and didn't have a lot of money to spare. I decided to spend just a little more money on a scale that I really wanted. It may sound insignificant, but that scale has always stuck in my head as an important purchase. I have cared for that scale, keeping it clean and out of harm's way. In return, it looks brand new, even though I have stepped on that thing almost every day for the last 15 years. Some days I didn't like that scale very much, but most days we are friends. There is no reason why my initial investment in that scale shouldn't last another 15 years.

The scale is just a small example of how taking care of your possessions can make the most of your money. Whether it's a large appliance or a small piece of furniture, get the most out of your investments by taking care of what you own. If there is a spill on your couch, clean it up as quickly as possible so it doesn't stain. If you have wood furniture, be willing to use a furniture polish on it occasionally to protect the wood.

The saying, "a stitch in time saves nine" is all about taking care of what you have. Consider it preventive medicine for your "stuff." If the carpet is starting to come up, repair it yourself or call someone in immediately. It could be the difference between a $40 repair and a $1,500 replacement.

If you can make your initial investment of a $1,000 dining room set last five or ten years longer than normal, that's $1,000 you won't have to spend immediately to replace it. By taking care of what you have and making it last as long as possible, you will also benefit the environment by not contributing to landfill. Finally, taking care of what you have also instills an appreciation for what you already own.

Top 10 Tips for the Home

---

1. Whether cleaning, making repairs or decorating, resist the urge to start more than one project at a time. By focusing on each task through completion, you will minimize the mess and chaos that can often accompany more involved projects.

2. Look for ways to make cleaning your home a more enjoyable experience. Blast your favorite music and sing along while you sweep and mop. Clean as fast as you can and make it a mini workout. Bribe yourself with 15 minutes of reading your favorite book after 30 minutes of cleaning.

3. Invest in a basic tool set. With the Internet at your fingertips, you can fix more than you think.

4. Expand your home beyond its walls. Utilize balconies, porches and backyards to create more useable and enjoyable living space.

5. If you have carpets, it is worth investing in your own steam cleaner. A basic machine will pay for itself in approximately three uses.

6. Photos are an inexpensive and expressive way to personalize your home.

7. Invest in a down comforter, down blanket and flannel sheets for your bed so you can turn the heater down at night. Invest in a down blanket for your couch so you can snuggle in and keep from cranking that heater up in the evenings. Candlelight will add to the cozy ambiance.

8. Use the power of scent. Smell makes a big impact on your emotions. Realtors have used this trick for years during open houses to create a pleasing environment. Don't wait for special occasions. Burn a scented candle or incense "just because". You can use citrus in the day to enhance awareness or lavender at night for relaxation.

9. Don't wait for special occasions to use your good dishes, serving set or towels. Put them into use on a Tuesday night or a Saturday morning. You and your family deserve to be treated as well as any guest that walks into your home. Appreciate and enjoy what you have.

10. Create a money-saving network. Be willing to share your steam cleaner in exchange for your friend's power washer. Borrowing is an excellent way to save money and reduce clutter by not having to purchase machines you may only need to use a few times per year.

Chapter 7

Entertainment

Sharpen the Saw

We all need rest and relaxation. We need a break from our normal routine to regroup and renew. R&R makes us better employees, coworkers, spouses, parents and friends. As Stephen Covey, the author of *The 7 Habits of Highly Effective People* advises, you have to take the time to sharpen your saw or you end up working with a dull blade. Enjoy your time off from work even more by being financially smart about your activities.

In this chapter, we will look at:

- Planning and enjoying your vacation.
- Finding money for your vacation.
- How to "get away" without leaving home.
- Smart planning to save on hobbies, entertaining and dining out.
- How to successfully manage social spending.

Vacations

Have you ever gone on vacation and had an empty feeling in the pit of your stomach the whole time because you knew you couldn't "afford it", or that you would be paying it off for months or years after the fact? Did you come back more stressed and exhausted than when you left?

The key to getting the most out of your vacation is to set aside for it in advance. Vacations aren't relaxing when you're piling charges onto your credit card and you know you will have to face the consequences over the coming months - if not longer.

Planning is the number one tool for savvy vacationing. By planning in advance, you are able to take the time to research and find the best rates. Planning also gives you the opportunity to save for it.

Carefully planning, if done in a positive manner, can be half the fun of the vacation itself. Planning builds anticipation. Anyone who has read the *Tao of Pooh* by Benjamin Hoff knows the anticipation of the taste of honey is as sweet as the actual taste. The same philosophy applies to vacations. The excitement of planning can be as enjoyable as the actual vacation.

The first step for planning for your vacation is to decide where you want to go. Next, identify when you want to go. Deciding when you want to go on your trip is important for several reasons. By giving a specific date you create a mental deadline to make that trip happen. Too many times I have caught up with friends I haven't seen for several years and they tell me about a specific trip they want to go on next year. This trip is the same one I have heard them talk about for the last 10 years. The problem with making a statement like, "next year" is that "next year" is always one year from today. Instead, make a statement such as, "I am going to Australia on July 11, 2014." Even if you don't hit the exact date, you are likely to be far closer than if you continued saying "next year".

The second reason you want to plan a specific date is the time of year you go will directly impact your experience during the trip. Plan a vacation in Paris during August and you may be disappointed as a large percentage of Parisians head out of town during that month. Visit Disney World in June and you will be waiting in long lines in the hot Florida sun, as summer is peak season for the resort.

Paul and I do not enjoy crowds, especially when traveling with Dante. Whenever possible, we try to plan our travel during the off season. Occasionally, that means the weather isn't as good, but that doesn't bother us. We would rather wear an extra layer of clothing, than fight crowds wherever we go. In addition, by traveling off season, we save hundreds of dollars on air and hotel fees. For us, it's a win-win preference.

Once you have decided where and when you want to go, it's time to do the fun part - research! Thanks to the Internet, the amount of free information for travel is limitless, so it is the best place to start. For example, *Budget Travel* magazine's website (www.budgettravel.com) is a valuable, up-to-date resource. Specifically, The Real Deal section at Budget Travel is filled with their editors' picks of the best travel deals and vacation packages world-wide.

For those visiting Europe, Rick Steves is the go-to-travel-guy. His website (www.ricksteves.com) is filled with information including a Plan Your Trip page. If you have a chance to catch one of his shows on PBS, it will fuel your anticipation.

Lonely Planet is another excellent resource. Their website (www. lonelyplanet.com) and books are filled with travel advice, tips and destination information to inspire you. The photos posted on their website will whet your appetite for your own pending adventures.

Once you have exhausted the Internet, you can check out the library for books on your destination. If you are like me and enjoy adding travel books to your library, then invest in your own. I have had great luck getting used travel books through PaperBackSwap.com.

Some of the best tips I have received for destinations came from friends. As we planned our trip to Scotland, our friends highly recommended a visit to Orkney. I wasn't as excited about it at the time, but am grateful to this day for their recommendation. Orkney, and specifically the Ring of Brodgar is one of my favorite places on earth. I never would have gone there if it wasn't recommended to me.

When it comes to actually booking your trip, the Internet is filled with websites competing for your attention. One of my favorites is Kayak.com. Living in the San Francisco Bay Area, Paul and I are lucky to be within 30 minutes of three international airports. Kayak.com allows me to easily research prices at the various airports without having to re-enter the information each time. What used to take me 30 - 60 minutes to research now only takes 10 - 15 minutes.

Although online travel sites are easy to use, there are situations where it pays to use a travel agent. During an interview with Jay D'Amato, the Director of Leisure Travel at Smart Travel in San Francisco, I learned that even if you have budget constraints, working with an agent is a smart move. When booking travel online, you often purchase separate components of your trip and it's too easy to exceed your budget. In working with an agent, they figure out how much your trip is going to cost you in total before booking anything.

Also, if you don't know the area you're going to, it's too easy to opt for a "just out of Rome" hotel room. Once you arrive, you realize it costs you $20 each time you want to go into Rome. Very quickly you have blown your budget and wasted time just getting to your destination.

Agents get information on a daily basis and can keep an eye out for you. Let them know what you're looking for, especially if you plan far in advance. When they are notified of a sale or price drop, they will pick up the phone and call you. A website is not going to call you.

It is a good idea to use an agent when you are traveling out of the country, especially if you don't speak the language. If something happens, whether it's a natural or political crisis, an agent can help get you back home.

Agents do not charge their clients. Vendors such as cruise lines and tours pay the agents. Airlines do not. If you are just looking for an airline ticket, go online and purchase it. An agent won't be able to get you a better deal.

There are so many different ways to travel and so many different ways to save. Listed below is a few of our favorite money saving tips on some of our favorite modes of travel.

Save on Air Travel

- We already mentioned traveling off season can save you up to 50%, sometimes even more.

- The most expensive fares are on Friday and Sunday nights as everyone tries to get in and out for the weekend. If you have the flexibility to fly early on a Friday morning and are willing to fly back early on Sunday morning, you can enjoy that weekend away for far less. The discounts associated with flexibility apply to other days of the week as well.

- Tuesdays tend to be the lightest air travel days, so if you can fly in and out on that day you can save significantly.

- If you are adventurous, you can take advantage of last minute deals by booking just a few days in advance.

- Sign up for just one or two frequent flier programs (of the airlines you fly with the most). You can combine the miles in one place instead of having smaller accumulations (that expire) spread out all over.

- When anticipating a foreign trip, try to get the most out of it by traveling on airlines that are in the same network, also known as codesharing. For example, many Lufthansa flights can earn you United Mileage Plus miles, as long as your ticket is booked as a United ticket. Each program has different rules with regard to earning miles on other carriers. Do your homework before you buy and you can not only save big, but you might earn big, as well.

- Hotel chains have frequent stay programs and many have an option of crediting airline miles instead of their points.

Want to save even more on your next trip? Eat before you head to the airport and keep an additional $10 - $20 in your pocket to spend at your destination. Depending on the length of your trip, you can save quite a bit on parking by having someone pick you up and drop you off. Just be willing to return the favor for their next trip.

Save on Cruises

Cruises can be savvy purchases. You can step onto a cruise ship and potentially not spend another dime until you get home. Your meals and much of the entertainment on the ship are free.

Taking advantage of last minute deals is an excellent way to cruise. Cruise lines need to fill those cabins. As they get closer to launching, they will drop the price and then you can pounce. One note, if Alaska is a cruise destination for you, you will rarely find discounted cabins. Alaska is only passable by ship from April until October and they almost always reach maximum capacity.

Repositioning cruises can be great bargains. When the weather changes in spring and fall, many cruise lines change the routes of their ships and will move them from one port to another. Instead of moving the ships without passengers, the cruise lines will greatly discount the cabins hoping they will make up that money in the casino and bars. In 2006, Paul and I took a two night repositioning cruise from Vancouver to San Francisco. The cost of the cruise was $199 per person. It would be difficult to plan a vacation for two people with hotel and food for less than that. To this day it was one of the most entertaining, yet relaxing vacations we have experienced.

The one thing to be careful about with cruises is the extras, such as drinks. With cocktails running about $12 each and the fact that you can charge them to your cabin, it makes it very easy to ring up a budget-crushing bar tab. Be mindful of what you put on your tab. Like cocktails, sodas are also a money maker for cruises. If you have a serious soda habit, check with the cruise line to see if you can bring your own supply on board.

As I mentioned, much of the entertainment on the ship is free. What can get pricey are the excursions. When Paul and I took Dante on an Alaskan cruise, we were shocked at the mark up. A visit to see the totem poles at Totem Bight State Historical Park was $39 per adult and $25 per child. It would have cost us $103 to go. Instead, we opted to not take an excursion while in Ketchikan and visited the Totems Heritage Center that was within walking distance of the dock, paying just $5 to get in. We also visited the Deer Mountain Tribal Hatchery and Eagle Center that was next door, then spent the rest of the afternoon exploring the streets of Ketchikan.

The excursion we did splurge on was the White Pass Scenic Railroad in Skagway. Dante and I both love trains and this was an opportunity for us all to take a three hour train ride through the Yukon and see some of the most breathtaking country in the U.S. At $125 per person (Dante was free) it was an indulgence, but well worth it. For us, it was the highlight of the entire cruise.

One thing to remember when planning a cruise is to take into account the cost to get to your ship. For our Alaska cruise, we were able to take advantage that the ship departed from San Francisco. Within 15 minutes of leaving our house, we were checking in. For our Vancouver to San Francisco cruise, we had to incorporate the air fare to get to Vancouver into the cost of the vacation.

Road Trip

Vacations come in all shapes and sizes. There is nothing like a good old fashioned road trip to get in a few days of rest and relaxation. There are many easy ways to save when traveling to your destination.

Keeping your car well tuned is key. If you are going on an extended trip and want to get your car serviced before you go, don't wait until the last minute. If the shop needs to do any major maintenance, it could impact your departure. Before you leave, make sure to check those tires for safety and to get the best gas mileage possible.

One of the greatest ways to save on road trips is to stay away from convenience stores. The markup can be as much as 55%. By picking up snacks for the road at the grocery store before you head out, you will make better food choices and save big bucks. It will also keep more money in your pocket to spend on treats when you arrive at your destination. Would you rather spend $5 on a soda and king size candy bar at a gas station or save that money for a regional treat?

If your car doesn't already have a GPS, and road trips are a big part of your lifestyle, consider investing in one. A good GPS can be purchased for as little as $150. We travel by car almost one weekend a month and finally purchased a navigation system. In addition to being used as a GPS, it tells us where the next gas station is and also helps find restaurants, liberating us from the options that are only visible from the freeway.

How to Take a Staycation

Staycations became popular in 2007 during the gas crisis. That summer, people looked for ways to play tourist in their home town.

What do you do on a Staycation?

- Go to that museum you've been pining over.
- Visit a nearby town or neighborhood and explore.
- Go to a restaurant you have wanted to try.
- Check out shops you have wanted to visit.
- Rent an entire season of a show you want to watch.

At first blush, the idea of vacationing at home sounds very easy. In actuality, it takes planning and a little discipline. Vacations are intended for a change of pace. While vacationing at home, it's easy to get distracted by cleaning your house, mowing your lawn or whatever chore catches your eye.

Just like a normal vacation, planning in advance will help you enjoy your staycation even more. Prior to beginning, thoroughly clean your house. Strive to make it as clean as a hotel or bed and breakfast. It can be hard to relax in a house that needs vacuuming.

Next, buy all of your groceries in advance. You don't want to have to run out for anything. If you plan on staying at home and watching every version of *Pride and Prejudice* ever filmed, stop by the video store in advance and rent them all. Do every possible errand ahead of time.

Once you officially start, DON'T:

- Turn on your computer.
- Check your email.
- Check in at work.

Why not practice taking a staycation by trying it for a weekend? Do all of your chores and errands before you get off work on Friday afternoon and spend the entire weekend relaxing and enjoying yourself. This concept may transform the way you look at weekends from now on.

No matter how you take your vacation, remember that it is the time to enjoy your experience. Stay within your budget, but be smart about *how* you budget. Be sure to allow for the experiences you will treasure such as a side trip, entrance to a museum or dinner at a particular restaurant. You don't want to make plans, take the time off and travel somewhere only to decide you can't afford to experience what you came there for. Just like we skipped the totem excursion so we could go on the train trip in Alaska, pick the memories you want to cherish.

You Can Take That Vacation

As I have mentioned, travel is a true passion of ours and a topic that comes up in many conversations. Sadly, too often I hear people say they can't afford to take the vacation they have been dreaming of. I have one friend in particular who has always talked about taking a week long motorcycle tour of Ireland. This is a serious dream for him. He has talked about this trip for over 12 years, but, whenever I ask about it, he says he can't afford it right now.

I know my friend goes out to lunch almost every day spending around $8 each time. He also eats out with his wife 2 - 3 times per week at about $50 - $100 each time. He spends approximately $40 per week on lunch and an average of $225 on dinner. That equals $265 per week, $1,060 per month and $12,720 per year.

Out of curiosity, I did a little research to see how much his dream motorcycle trip would cost. Note: All prices are current at the time of this writing.

- A round trip ticket to Dublin is $675.
- A Nice hotel runs around $95 per night or $665 per week.
- A BMW R1200 motorcycle can be rented for $875 per week.
- I budgeted $75 per day for food, totaling $525 for the week.
- I also factored in two pints of Guinness per day which adds up to about $79 for the week.
- **Total for trip - $2,819**

If my friend simply cut down his food budget by brown bagging three times a week and going out to dinner just once a week, he would be able to save enough money for his trip in just over four months.

Often we think we can't do the things we want because we don't have enough money. At the same time, we are bleeding money by mindlessly spending it on things that are not as important to us.

Finding Vacation Money

There are many different ways to pull together or earmark money for vacations and other fun stuff. One of the most powerful tools is to create a savings account specifically for vacations. ING Direct allows you to create multiple savings accounts so you can earmark your funds for a certain cause, i.e. vacations. One of the things I especially love about ING is that they also offer a checking account with a debit card. When Paul and I are ready to go on vacation, we transfer the money from our vacation savings to our ING checking account. We then use that debit card throughout our vacation. The money stays separate from our day-to-day checking account and we are able to spend as we please because we know we are only spending our "vacation" money. There is something very freeing about this practice.

If vacations are a big part of your life, start automatically depositing money into your vacation savings account. Even small amounts will begin adding up and will keep you moving toward your goal.

One of my favorite habits for "finding" vacation money is to save the money you save. For example, our grocery store is Safeway and we have a Safeway Club Card that offers additional savings for being a member (membership is free). When I use my card, the amount of money I saved is at the bottom of the receipt. When I get home from the grocery store, I automatically go to my computer and transfer that amount from my day-to-day checking to my vacation account. Through savvy grocery shopping, I save an average of $75 - $150 per month for our vacations. Also, the money saved by savvy shopping is used for a specific purpose instead of vanishing into thin air.

As you receive gift money, consider putting it into your vacation savings account. Do you get overtime? Instead of letting that money get absorbed into your checking account, immediately transfer it to your vacation savings account. Another option is to transfer any leftover money at the end of the pay period into your vacation fund. As you continue this process, you will be surprised at how quickly that money adds up.

One of my favorite stories about finding money for a vacation is that of my friends Gina and Kathleen. In January 2000, Paul and I informed our loved ones that we would be getting married that September at the Bellagio in Las Vegas. Gina and Kathleen started looking for ways to save money for the trip. Gina previously worked for Benefit Cosmetics and had a bathroom full of samples that she sold on eBay for a total of $400. Kathleen was a fan of Stila™ cosmetics and had a drawer full of their makeup. At the time, Stila was not available online. She was able to sell $200 of the product on eBay. With a little research, they found a hotel and flight package for Las Vegas that included four nights at the MGM Grand Hotel & Casino and air travel for both of them for $400. The money Kathleen made paid for her airfare and hotel. Gina made enough to pay for airfare, hotel and fun!

Whether selling your unwanted items on eBay, consignment shops or at a garage sale, the money for your next vacation could be hanging in your closet or sitting in your makeup drawer.

Discount Admissions

My friend Sophie is the Queen of finding discounts. She has a natural gift for pinpointing the cheapest tickets available. Because of this talent, she and her family are always able to attend the latest movie, play, museum event or exhibition.

Sophie has a ritual that she follows depending on where she wants to go. For example, if she wants to visit the San Francisco Zoo, Alcatraz or the California Academy of Science, she will first check to see if they offer a free day. Then she will see if a resident discount is available. Next, she will check if Costco is offering discount tickets. Through Costco, she was able to see the traveling King Tut exhibit at San Francisco's de Young Museum at a greatly reduced price, plus a free audio tour.

Finally, she will look on Craigslist to see if she can purchase tickets from someone at a discount. As a last resort, she will pay full price if it's something she really wants to attend.

Sophie also relies on Costco to purchase discounted movie passes. At the time of this writing, Costco offered five AMC movie tickets for $44.99 or just $8.99 per ticket with no restrictions or expirations.

In one of the classes I taught at Chabot College, I met a woman who easily could have been teaching her own budget living course. While raising her three kids, each year she and her children would pick one museum, zoo, or place of amusement that offered an annual membership. For that year, that destination was their main source of entertainment. They would go on weekends, attend all of the special events and get full use of their membership. The following year they would pick a new destination.

The Entertainment Book is filled with hundreds of 50% off coupons and 2-for-1 discounts, as well as money saving offers on travel and dining out. The 2009 edition for the San Francisco Bay Area offered over $19,300 in savings including:

- 173 dining discounts

- 55 attraction discounts

- 201 shopping discounts and more

Regularly priced at $35 - $50 depending on where you live, the book can be purchased for as little as $15 as the year progresses. *The Entertainment Book* is worth the price if you use it.

One trick my friend Lori does is to purchase *The Entertainment Book* that serves her vacation destination. During the first few days of a week long vacation, the book pays for itself.

Sports, Recreation and Hobbies

Traveling isn't the only way to enjoy your time off. The amount of activities and pastimes to participate in are endless. Do you have a passion for skiing? How about rock climbing? Are you an avid reader, movie fanatic or video game player? Do you collect antiques, garden or scrapbook? Regardless of what your passion is, there is a good chance that it costs money. Consider creating a separate spending account just for your sport or hobby. As suggested for vacations, if your hobby or sport is a big part of your life, set aside a certain amount per month that automatically goes into that account.

A specified savings account is an excellent tool for antique aficionados and collectors. Stumble on that perfect antique and the money is already there. Discover a great used bookstore and go crazy - you already have a book fund put aside. By saving all year long, when the snow starts falling and the resorts open, you have the money already waiting for you to go skiing.

The simple act of setting aside a certain amount of money each month and funneling extra money you receive into this account is an ideal way to enjoy your favorite activities - debt free.

Readers

As I mentioned, Paul and I both worked in bookstores and are avid readers. So is Kevin. In fact, we are surrounded by readers so this is a particularly important topic for us. We could easily spend thousands of dollars a year on books. Instead, we shop, bargain hunt and swap smart.

When I walk into a book store, I immediately head to the bargain book section. In addition to finding books for myself, this section is a gold mine of gift giving potential.

Paul is a big user of Amazon.com and will time his purchases to take advantage of free shipping.

We all love used book stores. Not only because the books tend to be discounted by 50% or more, but because of the variety. Mainstream bookstores keep what sells on their bookshelves and have to be very particular about their inventory. Used bookstores are an eclectic repository for excellent, unique, odd and even funny books. Also, most used bookstores will give you store credit for bringing in your own previously read books.

Like used bookstores, libraries often offer greater variety than mainstream brick and mortar bookstores and you can't beat the price - free! In addition to books, most libraries also lend DVDs.

Another free option for books and movies is to swap with friends. What I enjoy most about swapping is that I get introduced to movies and books that I might not have otherwise noticed.

Cheap and Easy Entertainment

Are you a movie buff? If you already have a digital video recorder, you can use it to record televised movies, reducing your DVD rental bill. By checking the television listings, I see what movies will be playing and set my recorder. I look for movies that I may have missed the first time around or ones that I want to see again. I've spent many enjoyable weekends catching a Cary Grant or Alfred Hitchcock marathon. You can find hours of "free" entertainment this way.

Wine tasting can be a pleasurable way to spend an afternoon. For the average price of $5, you can taste four or more wines, relax and take in the ambience. Even if you don't live close to a wine making region, there are wine tasting establishments popping up all over. A quick search on the Internet should locate the closest wine tasting opportunity to you.

As adults, we tend to think of entertainment as something you have to pay for - going to museums, dining out or catching a movie. There are so many wonderful activities to take advantage of for free or next to nothing.

We often forget the simple pleasures of an afternoon outside goofing around. If you are active, hiking or leisurely walking are free and healthy activities. Grab a Frisbee and a friend and head to the park. Have a pair of rollerblades in your closet? Dust the cobwebs off and go skating. In fact, challenge yourself to use every toy you already own at least once before paying to do an activity or entertainment again. If you have a closet full of soccer balls, croquet sets and tennis racquets, you may be able to play for months with the stuff you already own. Get your money's worth out of them!

When traveling I love checking out the unique shops and downtown areas of small towns. Even when home, I will occasionally head to a nearby city and walk around to explore. I'll find a coffee shop to sit and people watch or grab an ice cream or dessert at a local bakery. It's a cheap, fun way to spend a few hours.

The one good thing coming out of the recession is that it brought back family night and reintroduced the pleasures of the board game. My friend Lori and her husband are longtime, avid board game fans. Every Saturday night they host friends and play new games. They aren't the only ones who love board games. When I go out of town to visit my family, Paul has our friends Jesse, Kevin, Matt and Geoff over for a play day.

Growing up, my grandparents' small farm abutted ours. Just about every weekend a family member or old friend would come to visit them. Even as young as 10, I would love to sit and listen to them tell stories about the old times and just visit. My grandmother would serve coffee and a simple cake. The practice of visiting has gone out of style. It is a pastime worth bringing back.

Entertaining

Are you a party thrower? Do you love to host events and get-togethers? You can still do this and be financially smart about it.

Every party and event put on by a professional party planner starts with a budget. It makes even more sense for you to work within a budget. For bigger events, plan two to three paychecks ahead. First decide how much you want to spend. From there, create a budget for food, beverages, decorations and whatever else is important to you. Now, you know exactly how much you have to spend and can work within those confines.

Begin purchasing what you can ahead of time. Spread the cost over several paychecks. Fresh food has to be purchased very close to the event, but drinks, decorations, table settings and pantry ingredients can all be purchased far in advance. The beauty of planning ahead like this is it allows you to grab items as they go on sale or go to more than one store to shop for better prices.

Your event doesn't have to include a three course meal. Less is more and there is beauty in simplicity. Instead of going overboard with six kinds of imported cheeses, look for creative ways to serve simpler food. Take a class at a local community college or a gourmet food store on food presentation. Even little things like using salt cellars instead of shakers add a touch of elegance or novelty at very little cost - especially when you purchased those salt cellars at the antique store for a bargain.

Entertaining isn't restricted to having people over for dinner. Consider throwing a breakfast party. Breakfast can be made for a fraction of the cost of dinner. You can also have guests over for lunch or enjoy an afternoon of tea sandwiches and scones. You can host movie night with popcorn and lemonade, an evening of card playing with drinks and hors d'oeuvres or a late night of coffee and dessert. Your options for inexpensive entertaining are limitless.

Never underestimate the power of the potluck! For a long time I hesitated asking people to bring a dish when I was hosting an event. It took me a while to remember that all my friends love to cook and potluck events gave them an opportunity to share their favorite dishes. Equally, my friends who don't enjoy cooking are always excited to bring their favorite bottle of wine or a new beer they discovered. Potlucks allow your guests to contribute and also give you more free time, allowing you to enjoy your party that much more.

When it comes to serving alcoholic drinks, it's not necessary to host a full bar. Providing beer and wine that is paired properly with the food you are serving compliments the meal. If you would like to offer mixed drinks, offer just one or two types of drinks to keep your liquor costs down. In fact, this is one area that most guests are usually willing to contribute towards.

When getting ready for your event, it is tempting to buy new patio furniture or a full set of new wine glasses. If it isn't within your budget, apply the potluck idea and ask one of your guests to bring their extra chairs or wine glasses. If nothing else, do without. You don't want to have a financial hangover after your get-together.

If throwing parties is something you love to do, consider investing in hardware. You can shop thrift stores or sales for plates, silverware and cups to reserve just for your parties. After three or four events, they will pay for themselves over disposable and you will be environmentally responsible. Silverware and china will also add a touch of elegance to your party that disposable items just can't muster. Don't fret over trying to find sixteen matching sets of china and silver. Creative tables can be set by mixing different settings. In fact, using mismatched wine glasses can be an easy way for guests to keep track of their drinks.

Limitation breeds imagination. Often, the best thing you can do to spark creativity is to have to work within a budget.

Dining Out

Beginning in the late 1970s, Americans drifted away from cooking at home and slowly became more and more dependent on eating out. Our grandparents rarely dined out. Our parents dined out maybe once a month. Now, the average American eats out more often than at home.

In the first years of our relationship, Paul and I would wish we could go out to our favorite high-end restaurants. We would begrudge the fact that we couldn't afford the luxury. Meanwhile, we would go out two, three, even four times a weekend for meals. The places we were going to were chain, middle-of-the-road restaurants where the average bill was $35 - $50 for the two of us. We weren't enjoying the food, but we kept finding ourselves there or at a fast food joint again and again.

Why did we keep going out? Because our cupboards at home were bare. We couldn't seem to get organized enough to be able to consistently cook at home - and the sad thing is we both really enjoy cooking.

One weekend, after yet another mediocre meal out, we agreed to focus and start cooking at home. It took some trial and error, but by doing a little planning ahead and cooking at home, we now eat delicious meals for pennies on the dollar compared to the chain restaurants we once frequented.

Additionally, by cooking at home we realized for every third time we didn't go to one of those chain restaurants, we could afford to go to one of our favorite, high-end restaurants.

With the exception of our Wednesday Night Round Table Pizza Ritual (pizza is half off on Wednesday nights so our large, thick crust pepperoni and pineapple pizza is just $12), we only dine out about once a month. When we do go out, it's a special experience where we indulge in appetizers, cocktails, dinner and dessert. It's an event we look forward to and enjoy thoroughly.

Make your own dining dollars count and don't eat out because of habit or fatigue. Do it because you want to go to that particular restaurant. A friend of ours once said he only eats out at restaurants that can prepare a better meal than he can cook at home. This is a sound philosophy to follow. Why pay someone for something you can do yourself as well or even better?

You can save even more on your special meal out. Going out to lunch instead of dinner can save anywhere from 10% - 15% on your meal. Many restaurants offer discounts on particularly slow nights like Round Table Pizza's half off Wednesdays.

Most restaurants will also allow you to bring your own bottle of wine which can save you $20 or more. Keep in mind that they will typically charge you a corkage fee. You may want to call in advance to confirm and get pricing.

If you haven't tried it already, check out Restaurant.com where you can purchase a $25 gift certificate at certain restaurants for just $10. The coupon website often has sales in which some of those $25 certificates sell for as low as $2!

Don't be embarrassed to use restaurant coupons. The restaurant has spent money to have them printed as a source of advertisement. They want you to use them because they want your business. Check your favorite restaurant's website for additional coupons and special deals.

Remember - make dining out something you do for pleasure, not because you're too tired to cook.

Social Spending

A potentially money draining situation we get ourselves into is going out with friends. If you aren't careful, one evening can blow your spending money for the month.

This can be a tricky area, as your friends may be in a different financial situation or may not be as concerned with their finances as you are. Unfortunately, there is no one-size-fits-all answer for this one. As financial expert Suze Orman suggests, be honest with your friends about your intention of being careful with your finances. Suggesting less expensive alternatives or saying no if you don't want to go may be your best bet.

While it may be tempting, don't lie to your friends about your situation. There is no shame in saving money to spend on the things that are important to you. In fact, it is empowering. You are taking control of your finances instead of letting your friends influence your spending.

Note: don't get frustrated and think your friends can afford to dine out every weekend, buy new clothes and travel at will. As I said earlier, everyone's financial situation is different. They may not be as concerned with their choices. Another possibility is that going out on weekends, buying clothes and traveling is what they prefer to spend their money on so they save in other areas.

Regardless of their situation, remember, comparing your finances to the Joneses is dangerous. Don't do it.

No matter how you choose to spend your free time, have fun and be savvy.

Top 10 Tips for Entertainment

1. If you frequent certain airlines, sign up for their "deal alerts" emails and be among the first notified of discounted airfares.

2. Do you have enough clutter in your house to justify a garage sale? By investing a few hours of prep time and a weekend for the sale, you could earn enough money for your next getaway.

3. How many DVDs do you purchase? How many are still in the cellophane wrapping? If the answer is more than five - stop buying and start renting.

4. If you now feel bad about all those unwatched movies gathering dust on your shelf, sell them on Half.com! The same goes for books you no longer feel the need to keep.

5. You can also have your friends over for a book and DVD swap party. Make it an event with drinks and hors d'ouevres.

6. When going out to dinner with a large group, take cash in small bills. It will be so much easier for you to pay your share.

7. Think of ways to make simple pleasures even more enjoyable. Staying home to watch movies? Make a batch of popcorn.

8. Celebrate seasonally. Host an ice cream social during the summer. Enjoy an afternoon at the pumpkin patch in the fall. Go ice skating during the winter. Find a beautiful spot to picnic in the spring.

9. If you are traveling with a large party, consider renting a house together instead of getting individual hotel rooms. You will spend less on accommodations and have a kitchen to cook some of your meals in.

10. Take advantage of the free events your city puts on including outdoor movie nights, art and wine festivals and more. It's an opportunity to get to know your community.

Chapter 8

Wardrobe

Melissa's Story

When I first moved to the San Francisco Bay Area, I couldn't understand how so many of my co-workers could afford to buy new clothes every week. We were all making around the same salary and I could barely pay my rent let alone spend $100 on a new outfit each weekend.

Then I met Jessica. Jessica had a chic, adventurous style. This was at the height of the sweater-set boom when two or three of my colleagues would walk in and literally be wearing the same sweater set. Jessica never showed up wearing the same thing everyone else did. She had a tastefully edgy look and absolutely owned it!

I often asked Jessica where she got her outfits. On a regular basis she told me, The Salvation Army, Goodwill and vintage stores.

I soon realized another reason I was drawn to Jessica's look. This reason had nothing to do with the clothes she wore. It was her demeanor. She was relaxed and in control. She didn't have that "holy cow, I am $10k in debt and can't get out" look on her face.

Once I recognized Jessica's relaxed and in-control manner, I realized many of my co-workers were in hock. They weren't putting their finances first. Consequently, they were still paying off their sweater sets years after the sweater set look was finally put out of our misery.

I learned many things from Jessica; you don't need to spend a fortune on clothes to look great and style doesn't come from a mall. Jessica continued to be a fashion and financial mentor to me. At the age of just 24 she purchased her first house - in the hot housing market of San Francisco. Talk about saving money on the things that are not as important to you so you can afford to spend money on the things that are!

Our closets can be a maelstrom of physical and emotional stress. It's common for them to be bursting with regret-purchases, clothes that no longer fit but you are unwilling to part with and wardrobe orphans that don't go with anything else you own.

The average woman wears 20% of her wardrobe 80% of the time. That means 80% of her clothes are just taking up space, many of those items never worn with the tags still on them. In the U.S., it is common to shop for the sake of shopping instead of shopping with a purpose. We purchase clothes at random hoping the next item will magically pull our entire wardrobe together.

Your savvy mission is to create a wardrobe filled with clothes that look great on you and make you feel good. Your ultimate goal is to wear 80% of your wardrobe 80% of the time. Picture yourself going to your closet each morning knowing everything in there fits and looks good on you. No more trying on four items before you find one that is workable. No more sifting through clothes you will never wear, looking for one of the few items you put on at least once a week.

So how do you obtain this magical wardrobe? First, we have to start by diving into what you already own.

In this chapter, we will look at:

- Shopping your closet.
- Identifying your clothing needs.

- Organizing your wardrobe.

- Getting outside of the mall.

- Shopping strategies.

- The care and maintenance of your clothes.

Shopping Your Closet

It's ironic but true that the less clothing you have, the more of your clothes you actually wear. For this first step, you will need a full length mirror. If you don't already own one, you can purchase one for as little as $10. A full length mirror is a key tool to creating a polished look. Without one, it's too easy to leave your house with your skirt tucked into the back of your underwear. A full length mirror will also help you decide which clothes in your closet actually look good on you.

To start, go through your closet and try on every single item. Don't skip this part. It's imperative that you actually try on each item. Act as if you are in a store's fitting room. Decide whether or not you want to keep an item by asking yourself if you would purchase it again. Get very, very picky. Remember, the goal is to create a wardrobe full of clothes that look great on you and make you feel wonderful. If you aren't feeling so great in something, let it go.

As you go through the items, create your giveaway/sell pile, but also create a mending pile for those pieces you want to keep, but are missing a button or need to be hemmed. We will talk about what to do with your mend pile a little later.

Don't feel guilty about the money you spent on the items you want to give away. That is not a reason to hold onto something. If you feel really bad, consider having a garage sale to recoup some of your costs or try selling items on eBay.

Drawers

Once you are finished with your closet, go through the same process with your drawers. Examine your socks, underwear, lingerie and pajamas. Anything with a hole in it that can't be fixed, or that you know you won't fix, throw it away. Are the socks comfortable? If not, give them away. Is your underwear comfortable and functional? If not, get rid of them. Remember, no guilt!

Lingerie

Have you actually worn your lingerie? If not, try wearing the pieces you have at least once within the next 30 days. You don't need a special occasion. Whether by yourself, or around a significant other, wear your lingerie just for fun. If you don't end up wearing what you have within that 30 day time period, it is likely you never will, so consider getting rid of it.

Shoes

Are you holding onto shoes you will never wear again that are taking up precious space? Get rid of them. If shoes hurt your feet or you just don't love them anymore, give them away. Do you have shoes that need a little polish or to see a cobbler? Set them on your mend pile.

As you are going through this process, keep in mind that you're creating space for the new items you want to bring in. Think of your wardrobe as your own personal boutique. You want to be able to see everything so you can grab what you want and go. It's also a lot easier to get creative in pulling an outfit together when you don't have to shift through clutter and you can see everything. Again, stay very picky about what you keep.

Accessories

Go through your accessories with as much scrutiny as your closet and drawers. Think about the last time you wore a particular item. If it has been more than a year, it's not likely that you will wear it again. Get rid of it. A box of gently worn accessories is a great gift for a little girl with a penchant for playing dress up.

Jewelry

Jewelry tends to hold more sentimental value than clothing or accessories. With that in mind, it's likely you will keep more than you give away. Still, it's important to go through your jewelry and get rid of any items you just don't love anymore. If you have unwanted gold jewelry, depending on the market, you can sell it for a worthwhile price.

If any of your jewelry needs to be cleaned, pull those items out and take a few minutes to clean them. You will never have time to clean them right before you want to wear them, so do it now.

When you are finished culling your wardrobe, you should have touched, examined and reviewed every single wearable item you own. You will not have complete control over your wardrobe until you do.

The Empress' New Clothes

If you are on the verge of doing a complete overhaul with your wardrobe and want to replace everything, you may need to take the process in steps. It can make for an interesting day at work when you show up in your bra and underwear because you got rid of everything. Instead of purging everything at once, keep a bare bones wardrobe and as you purchase new items, immediately get rid of an old item. Do not hang onto it. It's like burning bridges. Don't give yourself the opportunity to turn back to your old habit of keeping clothes you don't love.

Inventory

Once you have gone through your closet, it's time to take an inventory of what you have decided to keep so you can create a list of items you need. Here is where it can get tricky. Everyone's needs are different. Knowing what to purchase depends on your lifestyle. If you are a stay at home mom, you don't need to invest in a business suit, but a few pairs of nice jeans and khakis will be worn on a weekly basis. If you work in a business environment, finding clothes you can wear to work as well as after hours will double the value of your investment.

The Internet and bookstores are filled with useful resources when it comes to building your personal wardrobe. Two of my favorite books are *The Lucky Shopping Manual: Building and Improving Your Wardrobe Piece by Piece,* by Andrea Linett and Kim France and *How to be a Budget Fashionista: The Ultimate Guide for Looking Fabulous for Less,* by Kathryn Finney. If you are struggling to decide what you need, both of these resources are a good place to start.

The important thing to think about when creating your wardrobe essentials list is what your weekdays and weekends look like. To give you an example, my clothing personality is casual with a splash of business. During the week, I can wear a suit for a speaking engagement or dress pants, heels and a button up shirt over a shell for a business meeting. On the weekends, I live in jeans and have a "uniform" of a funky t-shirt or a tank top with a hooded sweatshirt. I am not a shoe horse, but have recently confessed to a penchant for boots.

My wardrobe basics include:

1. Black wide legged pants

2. Grey wide legged pants

3. Dressy jeans

4. Every day jeans

5. Little black dress

6. Beloved vintage dress coat that my grandmother gave me

7. Warm waterproof coat

8. Cowl neck blouses (in three different colors)

9. Turtleneck (one in black and one in brown)

10. Warm brown sweater

11. Black dress boots

12. Western boots (for when I go horseback riding with my dad)

13. Classic black pumps

14. Black dress flats

15. Assorted t-shirts

16. Assorted tank tops

17. Black hooded sweatshirt

18. Assorted scarves

19. Assorted bracelets and necklaces

I also have an old pair of sneakers, an old pair of jeans and an old hooded sweatshirt that I keep to wear while doing yard work or particularly mucky housework.

I have a pared down wardrobe and wear 80% of what is in my closet within a two week time period. The list above does not include everything I have, but it is the bones of my closet.

You can see that I don't have any skirts on my list and the only dress I own is a little black dress. The reason is that I am not as comfortable wearing skirts and dresses, so I don't buy them for everyday wear.

Now is the fun part. Whether on your own or with the guidance of a book, website or trusted friend, sit down and create your own wardrobe essentials list. Think about the basics you need to get through your work week and your weekends. On your list you could include:

• Pants

• Blouses

- Dresses
- Skirts
- Shoes
- Jackets
- Underwear
- Bras

In addition to your wardrobe basics, be proactive and include clothing items to get you through a job interview, a last minute wedding invitation and a night on the town. These last three items can be budget and time busters. It's better to keep an eye out for them as you are shopping for the rest of your wardrobe than to have to run out and get them at the last minute, potentially spending more money than you intend and not being able to find exactly what you want.

Once you have created your wardrobe essentials list, make a separate list of the items you don't already own. This is your shopping list. Keep this list with you at all times. You never know when you are going to have an opportunity to pop into a shop. Also, the list will keep you focused on what you really need. Until your wardrobe has been rebuilt, do not stray from this list.

A Word about Pajamas

As you reinvent your wardrobe, why not also reconsider what you wear to bed? Investing in new pajamas (two sets so you can wear one while the other is in the wash) is a nice thing to do for yourself. You may just sleep better in something that fits right and makes you happy versus the hole-riddled t-shirt and ragged yoga pants you have been wearing.

A Word about Bras

Make sure you have the right bras to wear under your clothes. You don't want to be unable to wear a clothing item just because you don't have the correct foundation garment for it. Most department stores, such as Macys and Nordstrom, have staff on hand that can measure you and the service is free. Wearing the correct bra can make an outfit, but wearing an incorrect bra can devastate your outfit.

Professional Help

A wardrobe is very personal and you need to decide what works best for your lifestyle. However, for some, this can be very difficult to figure out. If that is the case, it may be worthwhile to invest in a session or two with a stylist. A stylist will not only help you decide what is missing from your wardrobe, they can also let you know what colors and fabrics work best for your complexion. While there is an initial investment, it will pay off over time. Once you know what looks good on you, you can save dressing room time by only picking up and trying on the colors and styles that work for you versus having to try on everything. You will also make better wardrobe decisions, saving money on items you thought would work for you while in the dressing room and realized after one or two wears they don't work at all.

If a stylist is out of your budget, no problem. As mentioned earlier, there are plenty of wonderful resources out there to help you educate yourself.

Organize

Organization is one of the biggest issues when it comes to limiting ourselves on the clothes we actually wear. Most of us don't even know what we have. Worse, because we don't know what we have, we often purchase the same clothes again and again.

Once you have inventoried and culled your closet - organize it! It will be far easier to organize your closet now, before you start adding to it. By the time you're finished organizing, you should be willing to proudly show it off to Martha Stewart.

One way to re-imagine your closet is to set it up like a boutique. Everything should be displayed in a manner that it is easily visible. However, everyone's brain works a little differently when it comes to organization. For me,

- I keep my clothes organized by type and then color.

- The clothes I don't wear on a regular basis are placed in the back including jackets and suits.

- I try to hang all of my clothes, including t-shirts. If they are in drawers, I won't see them and so I won't wear them.

Again, everyone is different and you need to do what works for you.

Once you have organized your closet, organize your accessories, shoes and jewelry. Your accessories should be easy to see and accessible. Perhaps you can place scarves on a hook on the back of your door. Purchase a hanging sweater shelf for your closet and in addition to sweaters, place all of your purses there.

Note: One of the shelves of your closet is a great place to keep a bottle of fabric refresher and shoe polish for quick fixes.

Consider placing hooks in your closet so you can hang your jewelry, making it easy to see. Most of us don't wear jewelry or accessories as often as we would like to (or we wear the same ones again and again) because we just can't take the time in the morning to hunt down what we really want to wear.

Know How to Shop For You

For most of us, clothing can be our friend and our foe. You may have one or two pieces in your wardrobe that make you feel great - and the rest are just "clothes". A closet full of clothes that look cute on the hanger, but not on you, drains your wallet and your self esteem.

Now that you have rid your closet of the clothes you don't feel good in, you need to figure out why you feel good in your favorites. Start with those one or two pieces that make you feel great when you wear them. Is it the neckline that makes you look good? The color? The cut? Once you figure it out, look for similar items when shopping. It's that easy! For example, I have three cowl neck blouses because an open neck looks good on my particular frame.

If you are still struggling to figure out what looks good on your body, an excellent resource is *Style RX: Dressing the Body You Have to Create the Body You Want* by Bridgette Raes and Lori Berkowitz. The title says it all. With more than 250 photographs, it helps you understand the proportions of your body, part by part, and offers appropriate clothing suggestions.

Preparing to Shop

Once you have inventoried your wardrobe and created your shopping list, keep it in your purse. When getting ready to walk into a store, pull it out and look it over. It will keep you focused on what you really need. Again, until you have completed or are close to completing your new wardrobe, focus your spending and only purchase the items on your list. Don't let yourself get distracted.

When it comes to systems of shopping, there are several schools of thought. When I worked in public relations, my boss Theresa would fly home to Boston at the end of fall and at the end of spring. She would do her clothes shopping for the year during those two visits. It would be a marathon weekend session where she would power through and take advantage of the end of season sales.

In contrast, Jessica would shop on a regular basis and haunt her favorite stores continuously looking for bargains. My shopping style is a little of both. Two or three times a year I go on an all day shopping trip with my mom. She always encourages me to try something on that I might have otherwise missed and go into stores I may not have thought about visiting.

In addition, I try to stop in at least one of my favorite stores each pay period. The stores I frequent include Macys, Old Navy and Ann Taylor. I have a favorite Goodwill store in San Mateo that I try to visit every few months and a vintage store in Fresno that I love to visit when I'm in the area.

Finding Your Inner French Girl

I have long admired the French for their sense of style, eating habits and financial savvy. Their shopping habits are worth noting and copying. The following quote from the book *Entre Nous - A Woman's Guide to Finding Her Inner French Girl* by Debra Ollivier, sums up their shopping habits:

How to Shop Like a French Girl

If she can't afford it, she won't buy it. If it doesn't fit (or make her feel good, or flaunt what she's got), she won't wear it. If she can't find it, she won't compromise. If she loves it, she won't toss it. She reuses it, rethinks it, lets it age.

When the French girl shops, it isn't a solitary act of buying something new. It's part of a lifelong process of editing her environment, making small but meaningful additions or adjustments to her home, her closet, her life.

When you shop like a French girl, you buy only one of anything - and make sure it's the best quality you can afford.

How can you argue with a culture known for their smart money habits and fantastic style?

Invest in Your Staples

We all love a good bargain, but when it comes to your wardrobe staples: invest. The "black trouser" is a good example of your wardrobe fundamentals and is an item that you want to last. You may end up paying more for this item but because you will wear it more often, the price per wear makes it worth your while. The more you wear an item, the more it makes sense to pay for it. You want to ensure it lasts.

A basic business suit that will not go out of style is worth the money for good quality. A trendy top that will be out of fashion in three months is not. Disposable fashion shops like H&M are good resources for inexpensive, trendy items that you will only wear a few times.

Once you have your basics and everything in your closet is wearable, then you can have fun and add other pieces to it. Just make sure not to purchase any orphans. Orphans are items that don't go with anything else in your closet. How many orphans did you end up with during your closet inventory? Strive to only purchase items that you can wear with the clothes you already have.

Professional stylist, Bridgette Raes, also believes the goal is to have everything you buy go with one or more things that you own. At the same time, she believes, if someone is looking to branch out, then they can buy something that doesn't work with their current wardrobe. Bridgette qualifies that statement by saying, "However, I always stress the importance of buying something that goes with the new piece in order to avoid creating an orphanage in the closet. Many people buy something thinking that eventually they will get around to buying an item to wear with it. That never happens and they're often stuck with clothing with tags still attached... hence the birth of an orphan."

Many orphaned clothes never find a mate and end up in your giveaway pile. Sorting through orphans every morning takes up precious time. Remember, your goal is to be able to fill your closet with clothes that you wear 80% of the time.

Avoiding orphans is especially important if you have purged the majority of your closet and are starting from square one. It is imperative at this stage that every piece of clothing pulls its weight. Set up rules. In order for an item to be allowed into your closet, it has to be able to go with something you already own.

Get Out of the Mall

Be willing to take an occasional break from the mall. Thrift, consignment and vintage shops aren't just about getting clothes cheap. They offer variety that you won't get with chain stores like Old Navy, The Gap and Banana Republic, which, by the way, are all owned by the same company.

Professional stylists say it all the time. Don't take a trend or someone else's style and copy it exactly. Take elements of that look and make it your own. Getting outside of the mall and shopping at second-hand shops or boutiques - where everyone else isn't shopping - is a great way to start.

"Fashion is something you buy, style is something you own!"
— Carine Roitfeld, Editor-in-Chief, French Vogue

Thrift Store Strategies

Thrift stores can be overwhelming. They aren't always organized like traditional stores and it can be tough to know where to begin. My number one strategy is to shop first thing in the morning. Typically, the store was straightened the previous evening and is still orderly. Also, you have a much better chance of getting quick access to a changing room in the morning.

Don't wander around. Start at one end of the store and systematically go through each rack. As you try on clothes, give them a close inspection. Pieces with stains or tears are not worth investing in. However, if you fall in love with an item, be willing to repair a seam that is coming apart or to replace a button.

One of the things I love about thrift store shopping is that it gives you the opportunity to try out clothes that you normally wouldn't. Find a funky jacket that is regularly $150 for just $10. Invest the $10 and see how comfortable you are wearing it over the next few months. If you find that it mainly stays in your closet, consider that $10 an investment in experimentation and get rid of the jacket. Now you know for sure that style is just not for you.

Remember, if you are in the process of rebuilding your wardrobe, stick to your list first and don't purchase that "funky jacket." You can experiment after you have restocked your basics.

One word of caution about shopping at thrift stores: because their clothes cost a fraction of what you would normally pay, it is very easy to overbuy. Whether you are purchasing clothes at a thrift store or a department store, it is imperative that you only bring home items that you love and look good on you.

Outlet Store Strategies

Outlet stores carry overstocked first run items, discontinued pieces and irregulars. Those who are on the far sides of the size scale, either XS or XL, can score big at outlets.

If possible, shop midweek for the best selection with the least crowds. If you can't find what you are looking for, some stores will special order an item for you and ship it free. It is worth asking about.

If you are loyal to a particular brand, see if the outlet store offers a frequent shopper card. Often, you can get even deeper discounts on the already discounted items.

A Guide to Vintage

When it comes to clothes, the term "vintage" means anything made from the 1920s to the mid 1970s. "Antique" means anything made before 1920 and it also means pricey!

If you like the idea of vintage clothing but can't figure out how to make it work for your wardrobe, consider finding a vintage dress as your go-to outfit for special occasions.

For the best prices, look for vintage pieces at flea markets, online or in thrift stores. Otherwise you will pay for the "vintage" label.

Go to the vintage stores for the education (it doesn't cost anything to look and ask questions), but once you know what you are looking for, shop for the bargains.

When buying online, make sure to get the actual measurements of the item, not just the size. A size six vintage dress is much smaller than a size six dress made today.

Consignment Shop Strategies

Although the items sold at consignment shops are used, the quality throughout the store is better than thrift stores. Thrift stores are comprised of donations. Consignment stores are comprised of goods for resale where the store and the seller both profit. Consignment shop owners are typically very picky about what they carry and look for quality items that are still in excellent shape. This extra attention means their prices will be higher than at thrift stores. Still, they will be far less expensive than brand new.

Consignment shops are great for finding clothes for work including business suits. You can even find wedding dresses. If you aren't terribly sentimental, you can consign your wedding dress back to the shop after the event!

Garage Sales

I am not an advocate of purchasing clothes at garage sales because you can't try them on. The risk is too great that the items will be relegated to the back of your closet or immediately placed in your giveaway pile. The exception would be jackets that you can try on or clothes from brands that you are familiar with. If you know that Ann Taylor's size 8 fits you perfectly, then the risk is greatly reduced.

What garage sales <u>are</u> good for are accessories and jewelry. Just as you would at a thrift store, thoroughly inspect the item for damage before making the purchase.

Affordable Designers

In 2004, Isaac Mizrahi sparked a fashion revolution by designing an affordable line of clothing for discount retailer Target. Since then, fashion powerhouses have followed his path including:

- Vera Wang for Kohl's
- Jean Paul Gaultier for Target
- Karl Lagerfeld for H&M

What that means to you is that you can enjoy adding designer items to your wardrobe at a fraction of what it would cost you otherwise. The majority of designers offer limited edition collections. If you fall in love with a designer item, you may not want to wait until it goes on sale. It might not last on the shelves long enough to be discounted.

Can You Actually Wear It?

When shopping, make sure you have plenty of time to try things on. Take your time in the dressing room. Sit down, bend down and pretend to drive or type in the clothes to make sure they fit properly.

One of the elements of elegance is wearing your clothes effortlessly. If your clothes don't fit correctly (too small or too big), are uncomfortable or are in constant need of adjusting, then it takes effort. You should be able to put your outfit on for the day and not think about it again until you take it off that night. Clothes that make you look and feel great will be worn on a regular basis and not relegated to the back of the closet where they transition from being clothes to clutter.

Beg, Borrow and Swap

Once your basic wardrobe is set, a next step would be to purchase accessories for special occasions such as a clutch purse, a shawl or a bold necklace. In the meantime, consider borrowing from a friend. Even after you have created one or two complete special occasion outfits, it can still be fun to shop your friend's closet. Just remember to give the items back immediately after the event in the same condition they were lent to you. Also, be willing to loan your own items when your friend is in need.

Buying Shoes

Like your clothes, you should strive to wear 80% of your shoe wardrobe 80% of the time. Get your money's worth out of them.

Take your time when trying on shoes. Walk the full length of the store in them. If they are too big, too small or pinch at all, leave them at the store. Have you ever seen a woman wear shoes that hurt? She walks in a manner that is the furthest thing from elegant. Whether purchasing heels, boots, open-toed shoes or flats, make sure they are comfortable.

One of the things I like about Zappos.com is the reviews. I chose my classic pumps based on the comments people left about how comfortable they were to walk in. With Zappos' free returns policy, you can take your time trying them out to make sure they will work for you.

Note: Make your shoes last twice as long by not wearing them two days in a row. Having a day off will give them time to rest and air out.

Yo-Yo Dieting and Your Closet

My mom is one of the most stylish, pulled together women I know. All my life, my friends have commented about her clothes and how great she looks. Unfortunately, one struggle my mom has always had is her weight. For as long as I can remember, she has been a yo-yo dieter. Consequently, her walk-in closet was filled with sizes 8-16 and she was only able to wear 10% of her wardrobe at any given time. Laughing, but in all seriousness, she confessed to me that at one point she contemplated going out and getting the size markers you see at clothing stores to place in her closet.

In February of 2009, after seeing the weight loss success stories in the FFIT program at Fearless Fitness, she asked me for nutrition and exercise advice. She started focusing on eating more fruits and vegetables, whole grains and lean protein and incorporated occasional treats. I helped her create healthy habits around eating that allowed her to enjoy those portion controlled meals so much more. The tweak in her diet, along with falling passionately in love with the game of golf, has transformed her from a yo-yo dieter to maintaining a healthy and beautiful size 10 figure.

Once she got to the weight she was pleased with, I encouraged her to burn her bridges and get rid of everything that didn't fit. She purged her closet of three 40 gallon sized garbage bags of clothes. Now, when she walks into her closet she can grab anything on the rack and wear it. This saves her 5 - 15 minutes every morning and her self esteem is no longer beaten up every day as she goes to get dressed.

My mom's story is not extraordinary. It's common to have two or three sizes in our closet and trying on multiple outfits each morning to find one that fits is almost routine.

During your clothing inventory, you should have purged your own closet of any clothes that do not fit, whether those clothes were too big or too small. Do not hold onto clothes that are too small for diet incentive purposes or because you don't want to have to buy new clothes when you meet your weight loss goals.

My friend Jackie had several outfits in her closet that were too small for her, but she held onto them thinking that at some point, she would get the incentive to lose weight and be able to fit into them. Unfortunately, by the time she did lose the weight, the clothes were woefully out of style and she ended up donating them anyway.

Your clothes make excellent barometers for your weight. Europeans have long used the zipper syndrome to keep them in check. The zipper syndrome is when your clothes feel tighter than usual or won't "zip up". If caught in time, it only takes a week or two of mindful eating to get back to your normal weight.

In the April 2010 issue of *InStyle* magazine, musician and fashion icon Gwen Stefani confesses that the reason she works out is so her clothes will fit properly on her. It's nice to know that some celebrities also have to workout in order to look good in their favorite clothes.

Take Care of What You Have

Once your money transitions from cash to possessions, it's easy to lose sight of the investment. A big part of being savvy is taking care of what you already have to make sure it lasts as long as possible. We tend to be good about that with items we spend more money on. Why not put that same care into the top you got on sale at Ross for $12, making it last as long as possible?

Sometimes taking care of what you have is to not do anything at all. For example, it's not necessary to wash your clothes every time you wear them. Unless you sweat in them or you got them dirty, don't wash your clothes. Washing wears the fabric away. Instead, immediately hang the item and let it air out over night before putting it back in your closet. If you would like, spray a little fabric refresher on it to freshen it up.

I learned a lot about laundry from my mother-in-law. She washed everything inside out, including her kids' t-shirts. It decreased pilling on sweaters and wear on graphics. She also hand washed delicates and laid them out on a towel to dry so they wouldn't lose their shape.

Another way to reduce wear on your clothes is to use your dryer as little as possible. I try to just dry my clothes for about 10 minutes which helps get the wrinkles out. I then immediately hang the items on hangers to finish drying. Stop by our house on the weekend and you will often see a batch of clothes drying in the doorways. This process more than doubles the life expectancy of my clothes. A perfect example of how damaging dryers can be is found in your lint trap. Lint is made up of fibers worn off your clothes.

The nice thing about taking care of what you have is that it will cut down on your housework two-fold. You will get into the habit of immediately hanging your items after you wear them so they won't get wrinkled. Also, by not washing your clothes with each wear, you will cut your laundry by at least half! The ecological benefits are plentiful as well. By not washing your clothes as often, you will save water and electricity. Additionally, you won't have to replace your clothing as often, saving on landfill space and avoiding the need for added resources to replace the item.

With the exception of your little black dress and business suits, avoid buying dry clean only clothes. In addition to the cost of having the items cleaned, you will reduce the hassle of having to pick up and drop them off. Also, you won't have clothes in limbo waiting until the next time you can get to the cleaners. By purchasing only machine washable clothes, you will be able to attain your goal to wear 80% of your clothes 80% of the time because they will either be hanging in your closet ready to wear or in the next batch of laundry.

Mend

Mending is a habit that fell out of favor in the last 30 years as clothes became more disposable. Instead of fixing a button we would just throw away or donate the item. Mending is a simple, easy to learn skill that can keep your clothes in rotation for years.

Invest in a basic sewing kit and the minute a button starts to fail, repair it. Make it a habit to mend what you can within a week. The perfect time to repair an item is while sitting at home watching TV. It will take you more time to pull your sewing kit out than it will take you to do the mend. If you have never sewed or mended before, the Internet is an excellent resource of how-to articles and videos.

For those items that need professional help, put them in your car so you will have them the next time you are in your tailor's neighborhood. If you have a lot of items that need mending, take just one or two each pay period.

This will spread the cost of your repairs across multiple paychecks. As you pick an item up, you can drop the next round off. When you take items to the tailor after they have been sitting around for awhile, it's like having brand new clothes for the cost of a hem or minor repair.

Cobbler

Forty years ago, a shoe was mended, repaired and as a last straw, replaced. Now, if a cap falls off a heel, the owner throws it away and purchases a new pair. A good cobbler can give your shoes new life. Heels can be replaced, stitching renewed and tears repaired. Leather can be revitalized with cleaning and conditioning.

If you have shoes that could use the care of a professional, bag them up and put them in your car. When the opportunity arises to take them to the cobbler, you will be all set. Being able to bring those shoes back into your clothing repertoire will be like having a brand new pair.

Do any of your shoes just need a little love? Take a few minutes and give them that love. Armed with a bottle of shoe polish, I owned and wore a beloved pair of classic heels for 15 years, re-heeling them just once.

Make it a habit to inspect your shoes as you take them off each night. If they need to be cleaned or touched up with polish, do it then and there. This is another habit that will allow you to wear 80% of your shoes 80% of the time as you won't keep passing over a pair because they need to be polished and you just don't have time in the morning.

Savvy Wardrobe Tools

During this chapter, we discussed many tools to help keep your wardrobe in top condition. Investing in these items will complete your wardrobe tool kit and prepare you for just about any clothing event or emergency.

- Full length mirror
- Shoe polish

- Fabric refresher

- Lint remover

- Hanging sweater shelf

- Shoe hanger

- Basic sewing kit

  ◊ Needles

  ◊ Thread

  ◊ Fabric scissors

Note: Add to your sewing kit as needed. Don't be tempted to invest in a lot of sewing doo-dads you may never need.

There is a confidence a woman exudes when she feels good in the clothes she is wearing. Strive to build a wardrobe that effortlessly allows you this confidence every day of the week.

Top 10 Tips for Your Wardrobe

---

1. Ask a sales clerk if they are aware of any upcoming sales. If so, it may be worth your while to postpone your purchase until the sale.

2. Sign up for your favorite store's mailing list. You will get a heads up on sales and coupons.

3. When shopping, head straight to the sales racks at the back of the store, then work your way forward to the regularly priced clothes.

4. Unless you really enjoy clothes shopping, do not do marathon trips. Take short trips and shop more often. You will be less likely to purchase out of desperation.

5. If you know that a size 8 at Ann Taylor fits you perfectly, try shopping on eBay. You can pick up clothes, with the tags still on them, for a song!

6. If fashion is your passion, set up a spending account for it. Kathryn Finney of *The Budget Fashionista* blog fame gives herself a monthly allowance for clothes.

7. Host a clothes swap party. An item you no longer love may be exactly the thing one of your friends is looking for. You can save money, have fun and be environmentally responsible all at the same time.

8. Create your own style book. Cut out photos of clothes you like and keep them all in one place. It will give you ideas for your next shopping trip.

9. It's rare that off the rack clothes fit every body appropriately. A good tailor can make the difference between just wearing clothes and looking polished. If something you own isn't fitting right, it may be worth the investment to have it tailored.

10. No one knows and no one needs to know that you picked up those great shoes you keep getting compliments on for next to nothing. It's not necessary to say how much you paid for an item when someone compliments you on it. Just smile and say, "thank you."

Chapter 9

Beauty

When it comes to beauty and beauty products, the pendulum swings especially hard between overspending and extreme frugality. We either make it a habit to pour money into the latest and greatest beauty products, or we are terrified to spend anything at all.

In this chapter, we will look at:

- Skin Care - taking a cue from the French.

- Creating a home spa.

- Drugstore versus department store cosmetics.

- Tips for getting the most out of your visit to the salon.

- Affordable manicures and pedicures.

Those French Girls Again

In France, as a rite of passage, a mother takes her daughter to an esthetician when she reaches a certain age. The esthetician will teach the young girl how to properly care for and maintain her skin. As the girl matures, she will continue seeing an esthetician on a regular basis, ensuring that her skin is kept as healthy as possible.

In the U.S., skin care is not the coveted ritual that it is in European countries. Makeup is indulged and revered. The unfortunate side effect of this American phenomenon is that improperly cared for skin ages more quickly. Too young, American women go from not caring about their skin to obsessing about it as they frantically throw money at anti-aging remedies.

Skin care products, from acne medication to wrinkle cream, comprise a billion dollar industry. Companies pour millions of dollars into marketing campaigns to get you to buy their products. There are many worthwhile products out there, but you can go broke trying to figure out which ones work best for you and the last person you want to get skin care advice from is the 18 year old behind the department store makeup counter - she is on commission.

Because everyone's skin care needs are different and should be evaluated individually, the person you do want to get advice from is a dermatologist. Most health insurance policies cover annual visits. Dermatologists aren't just for problem skin. When your skin is healthy, let them advise you on the proper skin care techniques for your specific skin type and perhaps even have them recommend an esthetician. As you age, your skin care needs will change. Annual visits to a dermatologist will keep your skin as healthy as possible.

No matter what your skin care needs, a dermatologist will advise a night time skin care routine. This is something I struggled with for years. By the time I thought about it each night, the last thing I wanted to do was splash water on my face. I just wanted to drag my tired body to bed. I tried to create a routine. I would be good for a few days, maybe a few weeks and then one night I would talk myself out of doing it because of fatigue. What finally got me in the habit is that I realized the benefit of giving my skin care products seven to eight hours to work while I slept. To help keep me on track, I will often do my evening skin care routine as soon as I get home - especially on the nights when I'm particularly tired. Occasionally, I'll miss a night, but I am much better about it than I once was and I no longer allow that one missed night to derail me completely. The improvement in the health of my skin is incentive enough to stay on track.

Once you visit your dermatologist and are prescribed a skin care routine, go through your bathroom cabinets and drawers and get rid of anything you will no longer need. Clear the clutter, just as you did in the rest of your house and closet. Time in the morning is particularly precious and there is no need to sift through half-empty bottles of old products to get what you need.

It's undeniably true that what you put in your body directly affects your appearance. Years ago, my mom and I spent a wonderful afternoon getting mud baths and facials at Golden Haven Hot Springs in Calistoga, CA. During my facial, the esthetician asked me about the dark circles under my eyes. I told him it had started a year before and that I chalked it up to getting older (I was 28 at the time). He asked if I drank coffee. I said yes, that I have two to three cups a day. I then waited for him to tell me to stop drinking coffee… which wasn't going to happen. He surprised me by asking if I drank it first thing in the morning before anything else. When I answered "yes", he said coffee first thing in the morning was making my kidneys work a little too hard, hence the dark circles. If I started my morning with water, then drank coffee, the circles would go away. I did as he suggested and within days, the circles were gone. That was my first lesson that what you consume greatly affects your appearance.

Removing as many processed foods from your diet as possible, along with increasing the amount of fruit and vegetables you eat, will improve the quality of your skin. Drinking enough water can be difficult. I gave up walking around with a water bottle years ago and simply commit to drinking a glass with each meal. That ensures I get a minimum of three glasses per day. Also, consuming at least one glass of water for every alcoholic drink will not only stave off hangovers, it will keep you from looking hung over. Be kind to your kidneys or they will rebel through your skin.

Every woman I have met who is over 40 and has beautiful skin has consciously protected it from the sun, including my 85 year old grandmother.

Grams spent a lifetime outdoors, having to quit school in the 6th grade to stay home and milk cows on her family's small dairy. My great-grandmother Vieira taught her to wear a hat while outdoors and wear gloves while doing more rough work like weeding the family's garden. Consequently, my grandmother has very few wrinkles and for as long as I can remember, she has followed a simple skin care routine that includes moisturizing with Oil of Olay™.

Hats and sunglasses aren't just fashion statements. They are tools for protecting you from the sun. Hats protect your face, scalp and hair from sun damage. Sunglasses protect the thin skin around your eyes from UV rays. They also keep you from squinting which goes a long way in preventing wrinkles. Invest in several hats and a few pairs of sunglasses. They are just as important as wearing sunscreen and are a lot more fun to wear.

Create Your Own at Home Spa

Like most women, I love spas. I take pleasure in the atmosphere and the personal attention. However, I firmly believe you shouldn't have to leave home to get pampered. Besides, it isn't always practical to go to a spa when your skin just needs a little extra help.

You can turn your bathroom into your own personal sanctuary. Not only can you indulge in a facial or foot bath anytime you want, but creating your own personal spa will entice you to stay on top of your beauty routine.

The main aesthetic in spas is cleanliness and a lack of clutter. Keeping your bathroom neat, clean and organized is essential. You can take it a step further and mimic the design elements of your favorite spa. A few simple ideas to add luxury to your bathroom include:

- An orchid
- A bamboo plant
- Several similarly shaped stones
- A palm plant

- Candles

- White fluffy towels

- White fluffy robe

Add another element to your experience by enjoying a pot of herbal tea or iced lemon water during your spa session. It will keep you hydrated and add a touch of luxury.

Creating your own at-home spa will designate a space where you can pamper yourself in just a few minutes a day. You can also set aside extra time to give yourself a facial, manicure, pedicure and scrub. This doesn't mean you can never go to a spa again. As mentioned earlier, your at-home spa will help you stay on top of your beauty rituals. It will also help you save money by allowing you to stretch out the time between spa appointments.

There are many good drugstore and department store brand facial masks that you can purchase for home use. Since everyone's skin care needs are different you need to figure out what will work best for you. Ask your dermatologist for his/her recommendation.

For thousands of years women have used warm olive oil to soften their cuticles, given themselves oatmeal and honey facials, sloughed their bodies with homemade scrubs and placed sliced cucumbers on their eyes. It isn't always necessary to invest in expensive beauty products. You can give yourself a facial with items in your own kitchen. Narine Nikogosian, the author of *Return to Beauty,* is one of Los Angeles' best-known skin care and beauty experts, with a client list that includes Jessica Alba, Charlize Theron and Alfre Woodard. *Return to Beauty* is filled with skin care recipes made from fresh ingredients that can be found in your refrigerator and pantry.

Drugstore versus Department Store Makeup

Did you know that Lancôme, a cosmetic brand featured at department stores and L'Oreal, a cosmetic brand distributed at drugstores are owned by the same company? Users of Lancôme's Juicy Tubes lip gloss ($18 a tube) and L'Oreal's Colour Juice Sheer lip gloss ($7 a tube), insist they are the same product. So why is the Lancôme product double the price? The answer is service.

Department store cosmetic counters allow you to try the different products. There is someone on hand who is informed about the products and can offer advice and suggestions. At the drugstore, you are unable to try before you buy. You can only hope the information on the package gives an accurate description of the color and use.

A little research can go a long way to make sure you get the most for your dollar. Paula Begoun's book, *Don't Go to the Cosmetics Counter Without Me, 8th Edition,* is packed with thousands of product reviews. A quick peek at her book will help you figure out what cosmetics are worth investing in, no matter where you purchase them.

The Drugstore

Drugstores are a particularly good place to buy "color" such as eye shadow, blush and nail polish. Like fashion, cosmetics are an ever-evolving industry. New colors, formulas and packaging are constantly being released. Picking up items at the drugstore allows you to indulge in a variety of hues and play with seasonal trends.

Again, the disadvantage to purchasing makeup at the drugstore is that you are unable to try before you buy. If you have a drawer full of "not quite right" products, start shopping at stores that have a cosmetic return policy. The price of makeup, even at the drugstore, adds up. You can save quite a bit over time by being able to return items that don't work for you.

The Department Store

Is there any reason to shop at the department store if you can get what you need at the drugstore? The answer really depends on you. One of the biggest advantages to shopping at the department store, outside of being able to try before you buy, is the opportunity to learn makeup application and techniques. It is amazing how a simple thing such as holding a brush a certain way can make a difference. Get your money's worth and pick the brain of the professional behind the counter for all the tips and tricks they can offer you.

You can also get samples at the department store which can save you from buying a full bottle of product that you later find out doesn't agree with your skin.

When shopping at the department store, take your time and cruise the various counters for a makeup artist whose own makeup you like. Tell her your budget and the type of product you need and ask her to help you apply it. If she is any good at her job, she will work with you. If you are happy with the results - get her card! When you are ready for another product, call and make an appointment with her. Knowing and trusting a good makeup artist is like having a good mechanic.

One tip I learned from Todra Payne of HealthyBeautyProject.com is to take your own hand mirror to the makeup counter. When trying foundation, add a strip of color at the jaw line that is recommended by the makeup artist. Then, add a color that is one shade darker on one side of the first line and a color that is one shade lighter on the other side of the first line. Wait a few minutes and then take your hand mirror outside to look at the three colors in the sunlight. The chemicals in your body and the air will change the color of the foundation. By giving the makeup a few minutes to adjust to your body and then looking at it in natural light, you will have a better chance of getting a makeup that best matches your skin. This will help reduce the possibility of a demarcation line which can ruin the best of makeup jobs.

Todra also recommends that you change your foundation with each season. Even with sunscreen, your skin color will become lighter and darker. It's not necessary to change all of your makeup every three months. You can continue to use your favorites.

One tip Todra suggests for inexpensively freshening your look is to put lip balm on, then add your favorite lip color. You will get a beautiful, barely there color that is not as heavy. You can also use a gold gloss over your favorite lip color, giving it a different appearance. For eyes, a gold shadow will look good over your regular shadow. Surprisingly, she said gold works on just about every skin color.

A primary benefit of department store cosmetic counters is they are very good about taking returns. When you spend $15 - $60 on a single item, be sure you are in love with it. If you get it home and it just doesn't work for you, take it back.

It's not necessary to be married to either drugstore or department store cosmetics. In fact, many professional makeup artists use cosmetics from both sources. Maybelline's Great Lash Mascara™ continues to be highly praised and used by professionals in both the film and fashion industries.

Tools

No matter where you get your makeup, the one thing you do want to spend your money on is tools. If you invest in a good set of brushes and take care of them, they will last for years. A quality brush can make a $1 eye shadow go on more smoothly. Todra recommends cleaning your brushes every few weeks with a mild soap such as Dr. Bronner's Baby Mild Liquid Soap™. This care will help them last as long as possible, making the most of your investment.

Application and Technique

The proper application of cosmetics is a skill that can be learned. Even if you're a natural, someone is always coming up with new ways to use a certain tool or inventive ways to use color. Just about every cosmetic brand offers video demonstrations on their website. You can even "Google" your favorite product to learn the techniques of the pros. YouTube is also an excellent resource and has an entire section dedicated to how-to and style videos.

Hair

Like skin care and cosmetics, it's very easy to drop a fortune on hair care. However, it's possible to have great looking hair and still be savvy.

When it comes to cuts, you can spend $17 at a value priced salon or $125 or more at a high end boutique. Where you choose to get your hair cut is a personal preference, but no matter where you go there are ways to save.

Can you change your cut so it's something that you don't have to maintain every six weeks? I prefer my hair long and one of the benefits is I don't have to get it cut as frequently. I only cut it every three to four months versus every six weeks which is often what is needed for short hair styles. If I pay an average of $50 for a cut, I spend just $150-$200 per year to keep my long hair maintained. My friend Jackie, who has short hair, has to visit the salon every six weeks. If she pays the same $50 for each cut, she is spending just over $400 per year to maintain her hair. Jackie's hair style is important to her so she is willing to spend the money. She stays savvy by saving in other areas of her life so she can afford to keep her chic short hair.

If you're in love with your stylist, ask if they would be willing to lock in their rate for you as long as you stay loyal. Before moving to the San Francisco Bay Area in 1994, I frequented a talented stylist named Ron Kausin who has since opened his own salon, Basics Hair Studio. I introduced Ron to my mom and my aunt who have both been clients of his ever since. When possible I try to squeeze in an appointment with Ron while visiting my family in Fresno. Ron locked in my rate and only charges me $40, the rate he used to charge before I left. In addition to appreciating my return business, Ron charges me the same as he did in 1994 to thank me for my mom's and aunt's business that he has enjoyed for the last 15 years.

If you really like your stylist's work, be willing to promote them. Ask if you can pass out their card. They may give you a price break for helping them bring in new business.

Another way to save big bucks at a high end salon is to become a hair model. My savvy friend Carla A. occasionally has her hair colored by an apprentice at diPietro Todd salon in San Francisco, CA. diPietro Todd is like a graduate school for hairdressing. The apprentices are licensed cosmetologists. Carla pays just $25 for a single process color that normally averages $85. The apprentice does all the work, but a professional stylist is there every step of the way to watch and offer advice. If she chose to, Carla could also have her hair cut by an apprentice for just $15. However, by paying less for color, Carla chooses to focus her beauty bucks on getting cuts from her favorite stylist.

Another tip from Carla A. is to ask for a "fringe trim". It costs a fraction of a full cut and may be just the pick-me-up you need.

Products

Hair products are another area of beauty that can easily become a black hole for your money. The trial size section of the drugstore allows you to invest just a few dollars to try new shampoos, conditioners and styling products.

Your visit to the salon is also an opportunity to sample products. If you like what the stylist used on your hair, ask for the name. Although, if possible, avoid purchasing products from the salon. The markup is dramatic. Instead, make your purchase at a beauty supply store or online.

If there is a product that you want to try, but don't want to invest in an entire bottle, visit that company's website. They may list where you can find trial sizes or be willing to send you a sample. If nothing else, they may send you a coupon.

Andrea Faria-Haze of Salon Techniques in Chowchilla, CA says she often has to tell her clients they are using too much product. "When people use too much shampoo and conditioner, their hair gets weighed down and they think they need more. It becomes a vicious cycle." Andrea suggests pouring just a little shampoo in your hand and lathering it up before applying it to your hair. It will be easier to work with. She also suggests,

"When using conditioner, only apply it to the ends of your hair. That's where it needs nourishment."

Think of hair products as investments. A little goes a long way. You seldom need to follow the traditional "lather, rinse, repeat" directions. I purchased a bottle of Frederic Fekkai's Protein RX Deep Nourishing Conditioner for $21. That may sound like a lot of money to pay for a single hair product, but it's the best conditioner I have ever found for my fine textured hair. I don't wash it every day (just rinsing it on the off days) and I only use a dab of product, combing it through my hair in the shower with a wide-toothed comb. I have only used 1/3 of the bottle I purchased five months ago. If it lasts me another 10 months, it only cost me $1.40 per month and my hair looks better than I ever remember. That's worth it to me.

My ever-savvy friend Carla A. splits bottles of products with friends, cutting the cost in half.

Hands and Feet

For some, a manicure and pedicure are necessities. However, if you can extend the time between professional appointments, you can potentially save hundreds of dollars or more per year.

The average price of a manicure and pedicure is about $40. If you go in twice a month, that's $80 per month and $960 per year. If you can cut down having a professional manicure and pedicure to just once a month, you can save $480 per year. To give you some perspective, that would pay for a two night repositioning cruise for two people from Vancouver to San Francisco - just by reducing your professional manicures and pedicures.

If you can extend the time between appointments even more and only go four times per year, at the change of each season, you could save $800. Eight hundred dollars is a nice chunk of change to spend on something fun.

One way to stretch the time between appointments is to invest in your own bottles of the polish colors you like. As needed, add another coat to help hide chips. You can extend that particular color for up to a week.

DIY

I like to do my own manicure and pedicure because I can do it when I have a few minutes versus having to make an appointment, drive to a salon, get them done, wait for them to dry and then drive home. I just don't have the patience to do it on a regular basis. Although, I do like to give my feet professional help at the beginning of summer and will indulge in a visit to the salon.

When I was a kid, my Aunt Sadie did manicures out of her home. I loved visiting and watching her work. I learned such things as how much polish you need on the brush for a good application. You can get the same type of education. During your next manicure, watch the details of how the manicurist works and ask questions. Most people want to be helpful and are flattered when someone is interested in their work. It's likely they will be happy to give you additional tips. YouTube is also a good resource for demonstrations on how to do your own manicures and pedicures.

Be Attentive

I learned an embarrassing lesson about staying on top of my grooming routine. A few years back, my feet were in pretty bad shape as I had not been exfoliating them or using lotion. To compound the issue, I work out at Fearless Fitness barefoot so my feet literally take a beating. I decided I was way overdue for a pedicure and went to a salon. As the manicurist started to work on my feet, she called over a friend to point out how thick my calluses were and they both started giggling. I was angry and mortified. At the time, I was too shy and embarrassed to say or do anything except sit there and stew. I left and never visited that salon again.

Within hours of leaving the shop I was laughing at the experience. My feet did look like I walked 1,000 miles barefoot. I promised myself to start taking better care of them on a regular basis and created a routine of exfoliation and moisturizing. That vigilance has helped reduce the amount of time I need to put into my self serve pedicures.

It's ok to spend money on your appearance. Ask any psychologist and they will tell you how you feel about your looks greatly affects your self esteem. A positive self esteem affects your relationships with your loved ones, your performance at work and your quality of life as a whole. The key is to spend your beauty dollar with discretion. Rethink your beauty routine. Be sure you are spending on what really works and not just doing what you have always done because you have always done it. Be willing to look for ways to save in areas that are not as important to you. At the same time, be willing to invest in areas that will make you feel even better about yourself. You're worth it.

Top 10 Tips for Beauty

---

1. For overall moisturizing, apply body lotion after showering, especially concentrating on hands, elbows, knees and lower legs. Remember to moisturize your feet, but be careful and don't slip!

2. Streamline your makeup process by only keeping the products that work for you. Don't waste time sorting through cosmetics, nail and hair products that you no longer want or need.

3. Don't let sales clerks intimidate you. They are trained to demonstrate at least three products to each customer and it's their job to up-sell you. Remember, they are on commission. Just pleasantly say no if you are not interested in additional products.

4. Keep your look fresh by going in for a makeover at least once a year. Know and stick to what works for you, but be willing to try new looks. Makeup is something that should be fun!

5. Consider having your eyebrows professionally groomed every other month and do your best to maintain them between visits. A proper

brow arch can make you look years younger and unruly brows can undo the best makeup application.

6. Remember to purchase cosmetics for your own skin color. What looks good on your friend may not look good on you.

7. Unfortunately, not every haircut works on every person. Texture plays a big role in how your hair performs. When looking for a new style, keep an eye out for photos of models that have similarly textured hair.

8. When taking example photos to your stylist, explain thoroughly what you like about the hair style. They may think you want six inches off the back when all you really want is your bangs cut similarly.

9. If you have a lot of beauty products that you don't want to just throw away, host a Beauty Swap Party for polish, eye shadows and blush. It's likely your friends are in a similar situation and would love to share. It's also a fun excuse for a party. Note: mascara, eyeliner and anything else used close to the eye should <u>not</u> be shared.

10. Sally Hansen's "Manicure in a Minute" is one of many products on the market that exfoliates, softens and moisturizes your hands and cuticles. They are worthwhile for those who don't have time for a proper manicure. There are similar, more heavy-duty products for feet as well.

Chapter 10

Food

Food is an integral part of our traditions, culture and celebration. Meals should be savored and ritualized. Unfortunately, hectic schedules, extreme dieting and not knowing how to cook have contributed to an uncomfortable relationship with food: how we look at it and even how we spend money on it.

Food purchases are the third-largest component of the typical person's budget (after housing and transportation), according to the US Department of Labor. Because of this high ranking it is one of the top areas to look at for reining in your spending habits. Cooking at home is one of the fastest and easiest ways to save money. As I confessed earlier in the book, Paul and I struggled with cooking at home because we weren't organized about keeping groceries in the house. By the time we thought about cooking, we were too hungry to go to the store and buy ingredients.

There's more to running an efficient kitchen than just buying groceries and cooking at home. This chapter offers a systematic approach to running an efficient kitchen in as effortless a manner as possible.

In this chapter, we will look at:

- Maintaining a food and supplies inventory.
- How to plan meals.
- Ways to improve your grocery shopping.

- When to shop at big box stores and how to do so effectively.

- Efficient kitchen management.

- Savvy and delicious meal management.

- Creating and expanding your cooking repertoire.

- "Must Have" kitchen tools.

- Adding more enjoyment to your meals.

Inventory

Everyone has different tastes and your idea of what is a staple may be different than others'. Create a list of everything you use on a regular basis. This will be a fluid list as you expand your cooking expertise and add new recipes to your repertoire.

Each pay period, or however often you go to the grocery store, grab this list and do an inventory of what you already have. Remember to include non-grocery items such as cleaning supplies.

Here is an example of our family grocery list. I have it organized by type of item. This helps me do an inventory in just a few minutes.

TOSETTI FAMILY MASTER GROCERY LIST			
Baking	**Meat**	**Beverages**	**Frozen Foods**
Corn Meal	Hamburger	Coca Cola™	Frozen Pizza
Flour	Hot Dogs	Coffee	Tortellini
Sugar	Steak	Beer	Ravioli
Brown Sugar	Chicken	Wine	Ice Cream
Chocolate Chips	Bacon		
Brownie Mix	Sausage		
Oatmeal	Stew Meat		
Syrup	Deli Meat		
Honey			
Shortening			
Baking Powder			
Bisquick			
Yeast			

Fruits/Veggies	**Dairy**	**Seasonings**	**Household**
Carrots	Milk	Taco Seasoning	Dog Food
Broccoli	Cream	Garlic Salt	Light Bulbs
Potatoes	Butter	Pepper	Dish Soap
Onions	Eggs	Mustard	Dishwasher Detergent
Garlic	Cheddar Cheese	Mayo	Toilet Paper
Seasonal Veggies	Jack Cheese	Ketchup	Batteries
Seasonal Fruit	Parmesan	Salt	Sandwich Bags
	Goat Cheese	Olive Oil	Laundry Soap
		Peanut Butter	

Canned Food	Bread	Pantry	Toiletry
Canned Vegetables	Wheat Bread	Rice	Soap
Chicken Broth	Wheat Crackers	Brown Rice	Shampoo
Tomato Paste	Cereal	Wheat Pasta	Conditioner
Tomato Sauce			Deodorant
Canned Tomatoes			Aspirin
Tuna			Toothpaste

I keep a copy of the list in the kitchen and we highlight items as we run out. Prior to heading to the store, we do a full inventory of the pantry, refrigerator, laundry room and bathrooms. This full inventory helps reduce the need for additional trips to the store because we are out of light bulbs or laundry detergent. It helps save money and just as important, time.

Once I'm finished, I decide what stores I need to go to depending on what's on my list. It's rare that I go to more than two places during one pay period. This list gives you an idea of what I often purchase at different stores. This varies based on each store's current sales.

TOSETTI FAMILY GROCERY STORE LIST				
Costco	Safeway	Target	Trader Joe's	Farmers' Market
Milk	Tuna	Toilet Paper	Goat Cheese	Carrots
Eggs	Wheat Crackers	Coke	Cereal	Seasonal Fruit
Butter	Bread	Dog Food	Beer	Seasonal Veggies
Yogurt	Chicken Broth		Wine	

Costco	Safeway	Target	Trader Joe's	Farmers' Market
Cheddar	Potatoes			
Deli Meat				
Cream				
Chicken				
Parmesan				

My store list has one big box store for buying things in bulk, a supermarket, a discount store, a specialty food store and a place to get fresh produce. I know I can get staples such as milk, eggs and butter cheaper at Costco than anywhere else, but if I only have to purchase milk, it isn't worth the hassle of going there just to save $1 on milk. Your time is as valuable as money. Balancing the time it takes to shop at additional stores with the actual savings is important.

The two stores I shop at most are Safeway and Target. If it's convenient for me to squeeze in a trip to Costco, I will, but only if I need enough items to warrant the time. I buy my groceries at Safeway and I buy non-grocery items such as toilet paper (or diapers while Dante still used them) at Target. I enjoy going to the farmers' market when I have time, but if I don't, I just buy my produce at Safeway and purchase what's in season and on sale. I try to get to Trader Joe's every six to eight weeks and will stock up on items while I'm there.

Planning

A common error when heading to the store is to buy "groceries". Groceries are random food items. Instead, focus on buying "ingredients". Ingredients are the components of a recipe. Planning out your meals before heading to the store will solve the problem of spending $200 on groceries getting home and "not having anything to eat".

Some families plan out breakfast, lunch and dinner. That's fantastic! For our family, the breakfast meals we enjoy are easy and can be made with the most basic ingredients. I don't worry about planning breakfast. I try to always have a deli meat on hand for lunches. If I have an abundance of eggs, I'll make egg salad to enjoy for lunch for a few days. What I do try to plan is at least four dinners for the week with the intention of having leftovers for other meals. How much you need to plan depends on you and your family.

One of the most powerful ways to save money on groceries is to plan your meals around the week's sales. Most stores mail their ads, or you can always find the information on their websites. If whole chicken happens to be on sale, you can plan to have roast chicken one night and chicken salad sandwiches a second night. You can also freeze the carcass to make chicken soup on the weekend. You have now made three meals or more for just a few dollars.

Another example is to time your purchases around the holidays. Pick up a second turkey at Thanksgiving. Place it in the freezer and in February you can enjoy a turkey dinner with all the leftover benefits. Before Easter you can purchase an extra ham to freeze and on a Sunday night in July you can enjoy a ham dinner. The following week you can make home-made Monte Cristo sandwiches, ham and cheese omelets: the potential is endless. I stock up on ketchup, mayonnaise, mustard and hamburger the week before the major BBQ holidays. With this process alone, I save big bucks over the course of a year.

In addition to planning your meals based on what's on sale, also plan around what you already have in the house. If you have potatoes that have been hanging out for a few weeks, incorporate them in one of next week's meals. If you have bread that's about to go stale, plan on serving toast with breakfast or French toast on the weekend.

Purchasing items that are in season is another way to save. You can get strawberries in the middle of winter, but those strawberries were likely shipped in, meaning you're paying for their transportation. Also, because the items are being shipped in from places as far away as Chile, they are picked unripe and never develop their best flavor or texture. Why pay more for poor quality? Pick what's in season, save money and enjoy. Your store's sales ads will be filled with in-season produce so it is easy to plan ahead.

Many newspapers have weekly sections dedicated to food. Some weeks they include an entire multi-course menu, or even a weekend menu with planned leftovers. Just follow the directions and you have meals cooked for multiple days!

Coupons

I am happy to use coupons when they apply to something I purchase regularly, or if I want to try a new product. However, the majority of food coupons are for processed foods. Because we don't eat a lot of processed foods I may only use one or two food coupons for each shopping excursion.

I do like to take advantage of coupons for cleaning products as well as personal hygiene and beauty items. They help me save quite a bit of money, especially if I can time them with a good sale.

The savvy way to use coupons is to only use them for products you are going to purchase anyway. Don't be tempted purchase a box of neon-green breakfast cereal because you have a $1 off coupon for them - unless you really like neon-green breakfast cereal.

Black Belt Grocery Shopping

Whether you shop once a week or every other week, put grocery shopping on your schedule and make it a ritual. Remember Savvy Habit #3 - payday is a perfect occasion for doing your grocery shopping. Do what you can to make it as pleasurable as possible. Take along a cup of coffee and wear comfortable clothes. If I am in a hurry, I hate grocery shopping. If have plenty of time, I really enjoy it. If you can get up, early mornings are a good time to get your shopping out of the way. The stores tend to be restocked and less busy. You can get in and out in half the time and you have the rest of the day to do as you please.

There's a Costco a few blocks from Fearless Fitness. I like to shop there after I finish teaching on Tuesday nights at 7:30 pm. Dante and I can usually get in and out in 15 minutes. Timing is everything. Ask the clerks at your favorite stores when the best times are to shop.

My inventory list is grouped by type of product. This allows me to do an inventory in just a few minutes. When I break down my grocery list by store, I keep like items together on the list. Those items are usually in the same section of the store. This allows me to go through the store systematically, greatly reducing the amount of times I have to go back to certain aisles because I forgot something. I especially appreciate this on the days I am particularly tired and just want to get my shopping done and go home.

Learn when your store restocks its inventory. Most stores stock fresh fish on Mondays and Thursdays, so buying fish on those days will get you a fresher selection than what you see on Sunday. Some stores bake fresh bread every *other* day. Knowing these schedules will get you better quality on the things that are important to you at no extra cost.

Most items go on sale on a six week cycle. Unless something is offered at an extraordinarily great price, pick up only what you need for the next six weeks. Sales can lure us into overbuying. Remember: your pantry is inventory. If your inventory isn't moving, then it's money sitting on your shelf.

Do you have a hard time getting to the grocery store? Consider having your groceries delivered. If you think $15 is too much to spend on delivery, calculate how many times you have to eat out in a week because there's no food in the house. If the answer is more than twice, it's worth it to have your groceries delivered.

Bulk Buying

Buying in bulk is only savvy if you use what you purchase. My father-in-law and my husband are no longer allowed to go to Costco by themselves. A small family does not need two gallons of olive oil, even if your last name is Tosetti.

When there is no wiggle room in our food budget, I walk into Costco with blinders on and only purchase the items on our list. If I have wiggle room, I will widen my focus and consider purchasing items that we haven't tried before.

One strategy for shopping at big-box stores is to go more often. If you only go once every few months, you have to spend a lot more money at one time in order to take advantage of the prices. Go every pay period or once a month and you can add to your pantry a little at a time. For my family of three, if I need to purchase a lot of basics, I like to go to Costco. I can get milk, eggs, butter, cheese, Greek yogurt, chicken and beef very inexpensively there. Other staples I occasionally need to replenish include: coffee, semi sweet chocolate chips and vegetable oil. If during one pay period I purchase the three pound bag of coffee, it only raises my usual bill by $12. If I wait and purchase the coffee, chocolate chips and vegetable oil at the same time, my bill would be almost $30 more than normal. By picking up just one or two non-regular items per pay period, instead of waiting to buy them all at once, it doesn't dramatically impact one paycheck. Instead, it spreads the cost of my groceries out, making it easier on my budget as a whole.

Remember to only buy what you will consume, and in the quantity you will use in a reasonable amount of time.

Kitchen Management

It's one thing to have a well stocked kitchen. The next step is to manage it efficiently. Start by consuming the fresh food you purchased first including fruit and vegetables. The most expensive food is the food you throw away. If you find yourself consistently tossing fresh vegetables before you can use them, switch to frozen. If you are worried about losing health benefits by using frozen, don't. Vegetables picked for freezing are processed at their peak ripeness, when they are most nutrient-packed.

If bread often goes stale before you have a chance to consume an entire loaf, keep it in the refrigerator and it will last a few days longer. You can also split the loaf and freeze half to use at a later time.

Chef Mark Parker of TheCulinaryWorks.com is one of my closest friends. I love to pick his brain and that of his wife and business partner, Chef Jennifer Whitmire-Parker about all things food. A few years ago Mark wrote an article for *The Savvy Life* giving tips for storing produce.

> Properly storing your produce will make it last as long as possible giving you more time to put it in use. Making a mental note of how your produce was stored at the grocery store will help as a guideline for how to store it at home. There are a few exceptions. Some items like apples, oranges and avocadoes do well at room temperature even if they were stored in the cold section at the market.
>
> Take everything out of the plastic bags unless they came prepackaged (like bag salads or bean sprouts). With loose items like mushrooms and green beans, roll the bag down so they are contained, but not enclosed. You want to ensure that air can circulate around the produce so mold will have no chance to take hold.
>
> Some items, such as onions, garlic, shallots and potatoes should be stored at room temperature and in the dark. If you leave them in the sun, they will start to grow and as they grow, they consume themselves. Potatoes also develop a bitter, green alkaloid under their skins when exposed to sunlight. Make sure you keep your onions separate from your potatoes. The onions release a gas which will cause the potatoes to deteriorate quickly.
>
> Many fruits will do better on the counter. They will last longer in the fridge, but they tend to lose flavor when kept cold. Check your fruit

bowl often and always add fresh additions to the bottom of the bowl. Also, store tomatoes on the kitchen counter instead of in the crisper.

When in doubt about the best way to store a particular item, you can always ask the produce manager. They will know the best way to store everything and might even have tips on how to best prepare things you have never tried.

Strive to finish your fresh food before pulling items from your freezer. At the same time, be willing to pull from the freezer before calling for pizza because you are too tired to cook. In our family, our goal is to cook or eat leftovers every night of the week - except for our Wednesday Night Pizza or when we have decided in advance to go out to dinner. However, knowing how unpredictable our schedule can be, I keep one or two frozen entrees for those "just in case" nights. I would rather spend $3 - $4 on a frozen pizza I can grab out of the freezer than $15 - $25 on dinner out and have to leave the house to pick up food.

Remember, the food on your shelves should be consumed. Strive to rotate through everything in your pantry and freezer within a three month period. At the end of each season (4 times per year), challenge yourself to see how long you can eat out of your pantry. Often, we get into the mode that a well stocked pantry needs to be static. If you see something sitting there for three months, either eat it or donate it to a shelter and don't buy it again.

Meal Management

Once you manage your inventory, the next step is to manage your meals. As often as possible, think in terms of getting multiple meals from every cooking session.

Last year, I had the pleasure of interviewing Chef Michael Chiarello of Food Network fame. I had wanted to interview him for a long time. I knew he grew up in the rural town of Turlock, CA, which is where my great-grandparents owned their dairy farm. I had read that his mother was an immigrant from Italy and I had a feeling he was raised in a savvy environment. When I finally had the opportunity to interview him, my suspicions of his savvy nature were confirmed. In fact, I walked away from the interview inspired and excited about my own savvy life.

Chiarello is a strong advocate of finding uses for food that might otherwise be wasted. A popular dish he serves at Bottega, his Yountville, CA restaurant is swordfish meatballs. The meatballs are made of the excess cut from swordfish steaks. This dish, made up of scraps that would have been thrown away in many other restaurants, is one of the most popular items on the menu.

Getting clever with your leftovers can help you invent your next favorite dish. Chop up remaining veggies and meat and stir them into fried rice for a complete meal. My friend Janna uses leftover veggies and meat to go into her weekend breakfast burritos. You can make the most delicious pot roast sandwiches from left over pot roast or hash with any meat and left over baked potatoes you may have. Your options are limitless.

You can freeze your leftovers in portioned packages which will save you time on a night you are in a hurry. A few minutes in the microwave or 20 - 30 minutes in the oven and you have a homemade dinner on a night when you probably really need it. Leftover dinners also make delicious lunches!

Don't think just in terms of leftover food, though. One of the most treasured items in the Tosetti family is a 100+ year old five-gallon vinegar barrel. Since before the 1906 San Francisco earthquake, Paul's family has poured the last of the evening's wine into the barrel where it turns into the most delicious vinegar. They use this continuously fermenting vinegar for salad dressings and marinades, knowing they are sharing in something created generations ago and continuing through today.

Getting into the habit of creatively using your leftovers will save you time and money. It can also inspire delicious meals that you may never have conceived of otherwise.

Eat Real Food

The less processed your groceries are, the less they cost, and the better they are for you. Be willing to do a little work. Full heads of lettuce are far cheaper than bags of salad greens. Whole carrots cost less than bagged baby carrots. A whole chicken can be 75% less than packaged chicken breasts. Once you get comfortable cooking a whole bird you will find that, in one cooking session, you have food for two to three meals, plus the fixings for homemade stock.

Cooking from scratch is far healthier and cheaper than buying convenience foods. However, remember to be willing to have a few frozen items on hand for those nights you come home from work exhausted. It will keep the pizza deliveryman at bay.

We actually took the "less processed food" to the extreme in 2009 when, along with six other partners, we engaged in "cowpooling." The seven of us purchased a 900-pound steer which we kept and fed on my dad's ranch for four months. When we had it butchered, it yielded about 550 pounds of meat (77 pounds per partner). Everybody got an equal mix of t-bones, tri-tip, ribs, filets, chuck steak, hamburger, stew meat and soup bones. After all expenses, including the original price of the steer, food, and butchering, the cost came out to about $2.64/lb. Granted, we had an advantage in being able to keep the steer on my dad's ranch, but isn't making good use of your available resources what being savvy is all about?

Once we get about half way through the original 77 pounds of beef that's sitting in our freezer, we will start the cowpooling process again. It worked out very well for us and our "steakholders". If you're interested in cowpooling, the Internet is the first place to start. You can join an existing cowpooling group in your area or you can contact a local farmer and create your own.

Family Cookbook

As you find recipes you and your family enjoy, print them out and start a family cookbook. You can use something as simple as a three ring binder.

You may want to purchase sheet protectors to keep the recipes from getting damaged. Even the cleanest cooks can get a little zealous in the kitchen.

The beauty of a family cookbook is the next time you are uninspired while planning your meals, you can refer back to your cookbook for ideas. It will also ensure that the recipes you enjoy cooking are in a safe place where you can find them easily.

Favorite recipes are like treasure. Over time, your family cookbook will become an heirloom. Several years ago I put together a family cookbook for my in-laws. I started by secretly gathering five favorite family recipes. I typed them up, copied them all and put them in "leather" bound photo albums. The nice thing about using a photo album is that you can add pages easily and the recipes are protected while you are cooking.

Each Tosetti family or family member received a cookbook. I then told everyone that moving forward, if they would send me their favorite recipes, I would type them up in the same font and format and disseminate them to everyone. It is an ever-evolving gift.

Cooking

As mentioned earlier, during the 1970's Americans began to drift away from cooking at home. The unfortunate side effect is that many children weren't taught to cook. As adults, the thought of cooking can become overwhelming. Luckily, cooking has come back as a pastime. We have gone from Julia Childs and Jacques Pépin teaching us the basics on public television to two channels dedicated solely to food. Cooking shows are now not only educational, they are entertaining. There is no longer an excuse of not knowing how to cook.

One of the best celebrity chefs to learn about cooking from is Alton Brown. Sit down and watch an episode of *Good Eats* and you will pick up helpful tips. More importantly, you will learn the science of cooking. Understanding the science of cooking goes a long way toward mastering the art of cooking.

Chef Jennifer agrees. "When I taught at a culinary school, I implored all of my students to watch Alton Brown. What he does that is so unique is he teaches the science behind how things work, how the technique operates and how to get the results you want. As a chef, it's most important that you understand these concepts. This information is key to helping you master a cooking method, and most of all, helps you obtain the results you want when creating or experimenting. For example, if you create a recipe using a béchamel sauce but it's not as thick as you like, you would have learned from him that the longer you cook the roux the less thickening power it has. You will know you either need more roux or less cooking time and can adjust your recipe accordingly. This knowledge is very powerful and he is one of the few celebrity chefs to teach these important basics!"

Cooking supply stores often offer free cooking classes as a way to demonstrate the products they sell. Each month, select Williams-Sonoma stores give free classes on basic cooking techniques.

Most community centers offer cooking classes for a nominal fee. They are a good place to learn the basics as well as more advanced skills like cake decorating.

Some Whole Foods stores offer various cooking classes. I thoroughly enjoyed their knife skills and cookie decorating classes. They were not free, but the fee was worth the knowledge I gained. Other higher-end grocery stores also offer cooking classes. Check with stores in your neighborhood to see if they have a mailing list you can sign up for to hear about upcoming classes.

One of my favorite ways for learning how to cook is to ask a friend or relative who knows their way around a kitchen. Offer to purchase the groceries in exchange for their knowledge. You will have an opportunity to ask questions throughout the process. Also, you get the benefit of a memory-making afternoon spent together and the enjoyment of sitting down to a meal with them after the lesson.

If cooking is a new concept to you, start slowly and commit to making just one or two meals a week. Take a basic dish that you enjoy and look up the recipe on the web. Many sites have excellent features where people can comment on how easy the recipe was, how good the results were and what helpful hints or changes might make the recipe easier or better. Be sure to check out these comments when researching a recipe.

As you increase your skills, consider cooking one or two more nights and double the recipe. You can use the leftovers for lunch the next day or dinner the following nights. As you get more confident, slowly expand your repertoire. You will find that many of the basic recipes are easy.

Don't worry about making mistakes in the kitchen. Even the best of cooks still make errors. Just a few months ago I forgot to put baking powder in my homemade corn bread and the results were comical - not edible, but comical! What you learn from those mistakes can be valuable lessons.

Hate Cooking? Assemble Your Meals Instead!

For some, no matter how much money they can save, they just don't enjoy cooking. No problem. It's just a matter of looking at it a little differently - think "assembly" instead of "cooking".

There are plenty of meals that can be assembled as opposed to baking, sautéing, frying or grilling. Chef Mark offers his take on the idea of assembling your meals.

Throw out your old ideas of traditional sandwiches. At its most basic level, a sandwich is something you can eat with your hands, consisting of some type of outer carrier (like bread) and some type of inner filling (like peanut butter or ham and cheese). Shake things up and be willing to try bread alternatives such as pita wraps, tortillas, French rolls, lettuce or cabbage leaves (think Asian wraps).

Sandwich filling ideas include leftover meat, chicken or fish. You can use sliced vegetables. Zucchini, eggplant, cucumber and carrots work well. High protein spreads like hummus are a delicious change of pace. You can even try olive oil, Italian spices, or pesto in place of traditional mustard and mayo.

Pre-sliced deli meat is the most expensive way to buy meat. If you really don't want to cook, you are better off going to a store that sells cooked whole chicken or roasts and cutting them up at home. Occasionally, you can get a good deal on deli specials, but still ask them to slice your purchase when you choose it, rather than buying the pre-packaged meat or cheese.

Salads are so much more than iceberg lettuce and Thousand Island dressing. One of the most interesting salads I ever had was an all meat salad. A salad is a collection of things tossed together with some type of dressing, usually served cold. It is another great way to utilize leftovers. You can use any type of vegetable, leafy green, fruit, pasta or grain as a base for a salad. If you are using uncooked vegetables, it is important they be as fresh as possible.

While I love all kinds of sauces, the heavier ones tend to overwhelm most salads. I always keep a jar of marinated sun-dried tomatoes in the refrigerator to add zest to my salads. Often my wife and I will make an entire meal of a fresh green salad. If you feel you need more substance, any cooked meat, chicken or fish can add body to your salad.

Technically, using a slow cooker falls into the same category of assembling food rather than cooking it. You just throw a bunch of stuff in the pot and let it cook for 6-8 hours. The key to making a stress-free slow cooker meal is the proper choice of ingredients. If your goal is to create a tasty "low-maintenance" dish, pick ingredients that won't get easily overcooked. Choose carrots, potatoes, turnips and other root vegetables instead of tomatoes and leafy greens like spinach. Use fresh sources for seasoning, like garlic cloves instead of garlic powder, whenever possible. The beauty of cooking with a slow cooker is that most of the recipes' directions are all the same: Put everything in the pot with some liquid and cook for six to eight hours.

Beverages

Beverages can be a budget buster, but if they are important to your quality of life, then there are ways to make them affordable.

Over the last 15 years I have had to come to terms with Paul's affinity for Coca-Cola™. Yes, I know we are in the health industry with Fearless Fitness. He enjoys it and it is important to him. Consequently, I can tell you where Coke is on sale and for what price on any day of the week. I know when it's an OK sale and will get one or two 12 or 24 packs. I also know when it's an exceptional sale, usually right before a BBQ holiday such as Memorial Day, 4ᵗʰ of July, Labor Day and the Super Bowl, and will then stock up on as many as the store will let me carry out.

Several nights a week, we like to have an alcoholic beverage with our meals. We're both big fans of dark beer and red wine. For a long time I didn't want to incorporate the expense of adding alcohol to my grocery list. However, I changed my mind when I started to realize that for the price of a single glass of wine at a bar or restaurant, I could buy an entire bottle for Paul and me to enjoy over several nights. Also, for the price of less than two pints in a pub, we could purchase a six pack of Guinness™ to enjoy for an entire weekend.

Our local Safeway has a very well stocked liquor section and our favorite bottles are often on sale. Another place I like to purchase alcohol is Trader Joe's. I can get amazing bottles of wine for $10 or less. Trader Joe's buys in volume, direct from suppliers, which helps them get better deals.

The Streamlined Kitchen

In February 2010, I teamed with Chef Mark to teach a kitchen management basics class at Chabot College. During the class, he pulled out his professional knife roll which contained approximately 12 different knives. From the roll, he selected three; a chef, boning and paring knife. He then informed the class that those three do 95% of the work and the remaining knives sit in the roll. That got me thinking about what we really do and don't need in our home kitchens.

I asked Chefs Mark and Jennifer for their thoughts on the essential tools the average American kitchen needs. As you read through their list, please note that it is meant as a guideline. Your "Must Haves" will depend on your own tastes and the type of food you enjoy cooking and eating. With that in mind, here are their suggestions in their own words:

Everyday "Must Have" Kitchen Items —
by Chefs Mark and Jennifer

Take a walk through the home section of any department store and you may notice the unbelievable selection of kitchen wares to choose from. With the ever increasing popularity of the home food industry, the number and variety of kitchen items can be overwhelming. A little thought and planning can help you approach your purchases with a keener eye for what you truly need versus what advertisements entice you to buy.

Having the right tool for the job is critical to the ease of preparation and having your dish turn out as you would like. If you are struggling because you don't have the right tool for the job, you will quickly grow frustrated with cooking and give up. We don't want you to give up!

As you can imagine, with two chefs in the house we have an extraordinarily large supply of kitchen wares. Too many, really, it's a bit out of control. But, if you get right down to the nitty gritty, you can create beautiful meals and desserts with the most basic accoutrements.

Day after day, you will find you use the same basic tools over and over. These basics are what we call "Must Haves". These items will ensure you can create most if not all the dishes you ever need without struggle. If this list seems overwhelming, relax. You don't need everything at once in order to prepare a meal. You should just consider completing this list before buying items that won't be used as frequently.

Pots and Pans

All pans should be oven safe and come with oven safe lids. This means no plastic handles! The oven safe option allows you to purchase fewer casserole dishes because you can also use the pans for casseroles.

- **10" or Greater Sauté Pan** - In a good quality sauté pan you can pan roast chicken or fish, make risotto, pancakes, scramble eggs, or even do stir fry.

- **Sauce Pan** - The sauce pan is great for making soups or sauces, warming up dishes or making small batches of pasta.

- **Stock Pot** - Stock pots are essential for economical cooking including soups, chili and so much more.

- **Cast Iron Skillet** - The old stand-by cast iron skillet is a Must Have for every kitchen. Not only should you use it to fry bacon or sausages for Sunday breakfast, it's the perfect tool for Friday Family Night burgers, gives steaks the perfect sear and makes the best fried potatoes ever. In our family, to bake corn bread in anything except a cast iron skillet is a crime.

When deciding the quality of pans to purchase, clearly your budget factors into the decision. We recommend anodized aluminum products. Typically, if you watch for sales, you can get some good deals. Also, you can find fantastic deals at wholesale professional chef stores. If you're not ready to invest in high grade equipment, look for basic aluminum sauté and sauce pans. They won't last as long as the higher quality items but they're inexpensive and can supplement your minimal collection while you build it up. They do a pretty good job and frankly, these are what are used in most restaurants.

Cooking Utensils

- **Spatula** - Spatulas come in metal or nylon, both being well suited to high temperatures. Be sure to select a nylon headed spatula if your specialty pans need the protection. Also, if your pans are non-stick, you need to find heat resistant plastic.

- **Silicone Spatula** - This is the plastic or wooden handle tool with the big rubber head that's perfect for mixing cookie dough or blending a sauce over high heat in a non-stick pan. These handy tools will not scratch your pans and they will resist heat up to about 500° F (260° C).

- **Tongs** - Think of tongs as extensions of your hands into unfriendly environments. They are also great on the cold side for mixing a salad and flipping food in your marinade. There are tons of designs out there but we suggest avoiding anything gimmicky such as locking handles or tongs that are described as multi-use. The extra functions will just get in the way and make it harder to properly use the tool. However, you do want your tongs to have springs.

- **Wooden Spoons** - Not only are they cheap, they are non-scratch and are good for stirring anything.

- **Potato and Vegetable Peeler** - Traditional peelers are called an "I" or swivel peeler and are great for straight jobs like carrots. A Swiss or "Y" peeler has the peeling blade attached across the "Y" of the handle and works beautifully on round shapes such as potatoes. They are inexpensive enough to have one of each. The blade will wear out over time so replace your peeler when it no longer functions with ease.

- **Mixing Bowls** - A variety of sizes enables you to do everything from whipping eggs to tossing a large salad. A set of smaller bowls can be handy for prepping and storing individual ingredients for later use.

- **Large Quart Size Measuring Cup** - These large measuring cups are handy for baking and can double as mixing bowls. Also, most of them have a pouring spout for those Sunday morning pancakes shaped like a certain famous mouse we all know.

- **Graters** - The box grater can take down whole blocks of cheese and shred a bag of carrots. This tool should be solid, durable and dish washer-ready since there is nothing worse than trying to hand wash something with that many teeth! The zester/grater is best for finer details such as zesting a lemon, grating fresh cinnamon from a stick or adding the final bit of cheese garnish to a plate of pasta.

- **Easy Read Individual Measuring Cup** - There is nothing worse than getting the measurement just right on the line only to realize that you were looking at the wrong side! There are lots of designs available, but we prefer the ones with bold markings and a tapered side that will allow you to more easily hit your measured mark. Make sure you have one made of glass if you are going to use it in the microwave.

- **Strainers and Colanders** - From hot pasta to chicken stock, both of these items are essential in the kitchen. Your colander is the easiest way to rinse and strain food such as vegetables or pasta. The strainer does the same job but with more attention to detail. In addition, you can use the strainer to sift flour, remove the lumps from a sauce, dust a cake with powdered sugar or strain the seeds from a berry puree.

- **Measuring Spoons** - We prefer non-plastic measuring spoons as they are longer lasting. It is worth having two sets; one for wet ingredients and one for dry ingredients.

- **Heavy Wire Whip** - From mixing liquid ingredients to whipping egg whites for a meringue, this is a mainstay in our kitchen. We have tried many of the "gadget" whisks including the nylon, flat and the ones with the little ball inside. The bottom line is that you want a whisk that is comfortable in your hand and is as large as you can wield easily. We can whip a pint of heavy cream to its maximum volume with one of these in less time than it takes to set-up our stand mixer.

Some newer whisks are available with a silicone coating over the wires. These are the best choice when used with non-stick pans. However, you don't need the extra protection if you use stainless steel pans and bowls.

- **Probe Thermometer** - This no fuss tool needs no batteries and can go from 0° to 220°F without a challenge.

Oven-Ware

- **Sheet Pans** - Find a wholesale or big-box store in your area and buy professional grade aluminum "half pans". You can bake cookies, spread brownie batter in the pan or even cook bacon on them, due to the high sides. They are inexpensive and last far longer than their fancy air bake counterparts.

- **Casserole Pan** - For baked pasta dishes or chicken and rice casserole, the big rectangular pans work great. They can also do double duty for cakes or other baked goods, like cinnamon rolls. Glass is the poorest conductor of heat so consider purchasing heavy anodized aluminum. The big pans they put on sale for roasting a turkey around Thanksgiving are great for this purpose.

Baking

- **Cake and Pie Pans** - Standard cake pans, spring form pans or rectangular pans are something you can collect over time. We recommend aluminum pans for long lasting durability as well as even cooking.

- **Silicone Mat** - Some people may feel this is not a Must Have item, but for the perfect cookie, coming from this pastry chef (Jennifer), it is required. They ensure whatever you bake doesn't stick and cooks evenly without over-browning on the bottom. It's worth every penny of the $20 price tag. Also, I purchase the generic ones. They are just as good as brand name mats and last for years. Keep them away from the stove top burners or they will burn.

- **Scale** - If you are a hard core baker, you have to have a scale. It's the only way to ensure your recipes are consistent every time and also allows you to use professional recipes. You are in luck as they are very economical. A $10 - $20 model can last for years.

Cutting Implements

- **Chef Knife** - There are a host of styles and designs to choose from but in the end, all you really need is a simple, good quality, all-purpose chef knife. It's important to find one that is comfortable in your hand and is the right size for you. We suggest keeping it towards the shorter end, 8-10 inches at most.

- **Boning Knife** - Smaller than its chef knife cousin, it allows you a solid grip and is small enough to maneuver between bones with its long thin blade and sharp edge. We listed a boning knife because we're hoping you will learn to break down meats like chicken, pork and beef loins as this will save you a lot of money in the long run.

- **Paring Knife** - Small and handy, a paring knife is used for tiny, precise jobs. They are intended to fit entirely in your hand for maximum control of the blade.

- **Bread Knife** - A serrated bread knife is a Must Have, because you can't cut bread properly without one. It can also be used for slicing tomatoes.

- **Cutting Boards** - It is worth purchasing several poly cutting boards so you can ensure they are cleaned between uses and you can save one for raw meat only. They come in multiple colors to make it easier to keep them dedicated for different foods. For added safety and to help keep them from slipping, anchor them to your counter top by placing a damp towel beneath the board.

Buying knives is an area where purchasing the best quality means you get the best results. Your investment will also last much longer. Many higher end brands come with lifetime guarantees. The best thing about high quality knives is they truly hold their edge longer, meaning they require sharpening much less frequently.

Invest in a good honing steel, to keep your knives sharp. If you don't know how to steel a knife, go to the website of the knife manufacturer for directions. When you purchase good tools, they give good results but you must take care of them. <u>Do not</u> put your kitchen knives in the dishwasher, ever. It will ruin the handle and shorten the life of what is arguably the most important tool in the kitchen.

Appliances

- **Kitchen-Aid Mixer**™ - Every pastry chef's pet, for all baked goods, bread dough, pasta dough... you name it.

- **Food Processor** - Handles everything from pie and tart dough to homemade salsa, grated cheese and pot sticker filling.

- **Blender** - Great for pesto, salad dressings, soups, sauces and cocktails.

- **Slow Cooker** - There is nothing like coming home to your house when your slow cooker has been simmering South American Pulled Pork or French Beef Bourguignon. It is an indispensable kitchen addition for anyone with a busy schedule.

These are somewhat high ticket items that perhaps, truth be told, you could do without. Their functions can all be done by hand or using traditional methods. But, the fact these items can make your life in the kitchen so much easier provides the possibility you may do more cooking at home. That makes them eligible for at least partial inclusion on the Must Have list. At a minimum, they can go on your holiday wish list.

Table Service

Gathering the family together over a meal is an important ritual of life. Again, not on the Must Have list, these items will simply make your hosting of an event a bit nicer. Being able to serve your dishes in an appealing and lovely way will make you proud of your efforts and make everyone else at the table feel the love you put into the meal.

- **Serving Platters and Bowls** - If you start with just a few in various sizes, consider sticking with a plain color so you can use them for every occasion. Once you have a decent collection you can invest in special designs for holidays, if you would like.

- **Serving Spoons** - You will find plenty of uses for regular large serving spoons and one or two slotted serving spoons.

- **Meat Fork** - A meat fork will be essential for those holiday meals that include large cuts of meat like roasts, turkey and ham.

- **Carving Knife or Slicer** - If you plan to entertain, this may become an important addition to your kitchen for roasts, turkeys or any other large meat item. The idea of a carving knife is that it has a smooth edge and a long thin blade. The lack of a serrated edge and the long narrow blade allows you to cleanly slice meat with one smooth pass. For occasional use, your bread knife or chef knife will work in a pinch.

- **Serving Tongs** - These are just nicer versions of standard cooking tongs, though not as durable for kitchen use.

Watch for sales and shop around discount import stores where you can find really nice items at reduced prices. Shopping just after a holiday season has ended is also a great time to pick up pieces to add to your collection at huge savings.

Gadgets

A key to determining whether or not a kitchen gadget qualifies for purchase is a positive answer to the following question, "Does it do more than one thing?" Any item that can only be used for one purpose, while perhaps fun, is not practical. Your money is better spent on either higher quality Must Have items or something that is more versatile.

For example, have you ever seen those cool avocado slicers? They're a good idea, but instead of opting for that, you could buy the higher end peeler which makes peeling produce (including that avocado) a much easier task. In addition, it can be used to create lovely peels of hard cheeses or even chocolate ribbons. Now that is a versatile tool.

When I (Jennifer) was in culinary school I was ridiculed by a French chef for using a blender to make mayonnaise because in the time it took me to get out the blender, set it up, use it, and clean it, he felt I could have grabbed a bowl and done it by hand. That may sound extreme but it's a good point. Do you need a gadget that makes whipped cream? No, it takes a few minutes in a clean bowl with a wire whisk. Do you need a gadget that chops an onion for you? No, it takes far less time and clean up, once practiced to grab your knife and chop the onion yourself.

Nevertheless, if you have weighed the cost versus the time savings you believe you will get and if a gadget makes the difference between you preparing your own dinner or going out - buy the gadget and enjoy using it.

A well stocked kitchen, complete with the items you use most often, sets you up for serious success in the kitchen. Not only will you be able to prepare food you and your family will enjoy but, by cooking at home more often, you will save a great deal of your hard earned cash.

Bon Appétit
— Chef Mark & Chef Jennifer

Organizing

As you spend more time in the kitchen, you will find that keeping it organized makes cooking a much more pleasurable experience. Professional restaurants are run like a military regiment. Every tool pulls its weight and has a place.

Now that you know the difference between a gadget and a Must Have item, go through your kitchen and declutter. Make it as easy as possible to find what you need when you need it. If your béarnaise sauce is starting to thicken, you don't want to sort through a drawer full of "As Seen On TV" thingamajigs to get the spoon you need.

The same goes for food storage containers. Invest in one set of quality containers and get rid of the whipped topping bowls you have been using. Everything in your kitchen must pull its weight and have a purpose. Although those whipped topping bowls are "free", they have a tendency to breed like Star Trek tribbles where they turn from container to clutter.

At the Table

Food is culture. It's tradition, celebration and a necessity of life. Meals should not be tiresome because you are being mindful of your spending. Even the simplest fare such as a stew can be made more enjoyable when served from a pretty serving bowl and accompanied by a glass of chilled water in a wine glass. A little thought put into how you present your food will add to the enjoyment of it. The restaurant industry has always used the art of plating food as a way to make their dishes more appealing. Why not put the same care into the dishes you serve at home?

Living across the street from my grandparents, I ate delicious and memorable meals in their home. I would set the table for my grandmother, usually with paper plates. All of the food would be placed on the table family style and everyone would help themselves. My grandmother was used to cooking for 10 - 15 people at any given time and unless it was a special occasion, the way the table looked was not as important as getting all the hungry farm hands fed.

In contrast, I remember the first time I had dinner at my in-laws. I was slightly intimidated by the beautifully set table with cloth napkins and candles. After accepting a before dinner drink, I was surprised that Paul's dad and stepmom Joan were chatting with us and not in the kitchen working on the meal.

When my father-in-law popped back into the kitchen and declared that dinner was ready, Joan walked to the dining room table and grabbed everyone's plate. My father-in-law then plated the meal. During dinner, we had our choice of a red wine or white wine. I was amazed at how delicious the wine tasted with the food. Prior to that, I had never had wine with a meal.

After dinner I helped Joan clear the dishes and chatted in the kitchen with her as she rinsed and put them directly into the dishwasher. She then made coffee and served a cake that my sister-in-law, who was 12 at the time, had made.

From start to finish, the meal was elegant and effortless. Here is the catch: it was the same delicious type of food I had enjoyed sitting at my grandmother's table. The simple additions of eating on dinner plates instead of paper plates, using cloth napkins and lighting a few candles made an enormous difference in the presentation and experience of the meal.

I later learned that when entertaining, my in-laws have approximately five different meals they prefer to serve. These are dishes they can easily make so they have an opportunity to enjoy their guests and not get stuck in the kitchen.

During my interview with Chef Chiarello, he made a similar comment about when he cooks for family and friends. He said, "If you are in the kitchen for two days before an event sweating it out and cooking with super expensive ingredients, and on the day of the event you are in the kitchen and not at the table enjoying the time with your friends, that meal will taste good, but you won't enjoy it. Turn it around and have Two Buck Chuck night and enjoy sitting at the table with your friends and that meal is going to have flavor because you are there to enjoy it."

That first meal with my in-laws was an impactful lesson to me that presentation can add immensely to the enjoyment of a meal. Since then, we plate all of our meals at home. I keep pint glasses chilled in my freezer. When I have beer, I drink from the pint glasses, rather than from the bottle. Occasionally, when I want a little pick me up, I'll drink chilled water out of a wine glass.

I still love going to my grandmother's home and indulging in delicious meals at her table. Although I prefer to plate my meals at home, I enjoy eating family style in her home because that's the tradition of her house.

While writing this book, my mom reminded me of a conversation we had when I was 15. I asked her why we never use our good china. She told me that we save it to use for company. I asked her why we couldn't use it just for us as we were just as special as company. In thinking back to that conversation, she mentioned that in the old days, your fine china and silverware was passed down from generation to generation and was irreplaceable. Also, for many, there wasn't enough money to replace an item if it was lost or broke. So, saving your "good china" for only the most special of occasions became habit. In this day, often even heirloom items can be replaced. Add beauty to your ordinary days and use your good china for Wednesday Night Pizza Night or any other special-to-you occasion.

Portion Control

The practice of portion control appeals to both my savvy and fitness lifestyle. It is not a secret that in the last 30 years, the average serving at a restaurant has expanded by up to three times. Unfortunately, those servings have followed us home and we often dish out twice as much food as necessary or we go back for seconds and even thirds. The simple practice of portion control will save you money and calories.

When dining out, make it a habit to enjoy half of your meal at the restaurant and take the other half home. You have saved yourself from having to cook a meal, you have halved the price of your meal because it has been split into two and you can enjoy that dish a second time.

The same can be done at home. Downsize your portions and don't go back for seconds. You will have plenty of food for one or two more meals. It reduces your time in the kitchen spent cooking. You have stretched the money spent on that meal into two or three meals and you can enjoy that meal a second or third time.

As a whole, think small. If you enjoy coffee drinks, instead of opting for the venti size Frappuccino at Starbucks, choose the tall. A tall Frappuccino with whole milk is 180 calories and costs about $2.95. A venti Frappuccino with whole milk is 330 calories and goes for around $3.95. Why not save $1 and 150 calories by getting the smaller coffee? I put it in perspective for myself that if I want to be smaller, I need to order smaller.

Although food is one of the easiest areas of our day-to-day lives to save money, resist the urge to become overly frugal. Strive for balance. Become a black belt in grocery shopping. Discover the enjoyment of cooking your own meals. Look for ways to make even the simplest of meals pleasurable.

"Nothing would be more tiresome than eating and drinking if God had not made them a pleasure as well as a necessity."

— Voltaire

Top 10 Tips for the Pantry

---

1. Find a big box store buddy that you can split your purchases with. Instead of having to find a place to store 30 rolls of toilet paper you will only have find space for 15.

2. When time is available, shop at a local grocery store or farmers' market for fresh food, a big box store for common staples, a discount store

for health and beauty items and a specialty store for less common foods and beverages.

3. Once you have cut back dining out, become pickier about where you go and break the monotony of going to the same places again and again. That's the fun part!

4. Just because something is on sale doesn't mean it's a good bargain - for you. If it's going to collect dust on your pantry shelf, leave it at the grocery store.

5. Keep your sink free of dishes and have a cutting board waiting and ready to use on your counter. The clean sink and cutting board is inviting and enables you to jump right into cooking instead of having to clean up before you even get started.

6. As your cooking skills develop, try making one new recipe a week. It's easy to get into a cooking rut. With so many free or inexpensive recipe resources out there, inspiration to cook is a click away.

7. Invest in a slow cooker! It will save you time by slowly cooking dinner while you are at work, plus it will save you money. The slow cooking process turns less expensive cuts of meat into delicious meals.

8. Invest in a dozen 2-quart mason jars and use them to store dry goods such as rice and pasta. They will stay fresher longer then if kept in the original bags and boxes. It will be easier to do your inventory as you can see how low you are without having to open a box and check. It will also make your pantry shelves look nice and neat. You can even use them in the fridge to keep your parsley, basil and cilantro fresh. They will last twice as long if stored with water.

9. Create a price book. Keep the average prices and the sale prices of your regularly purchased items there, so you know when it's a real deal. Include the "per unit" price as well, so that you can more easily compare different sized containers. This is especially useful when comparing between big-box stores and regular grocery stores.

10. Decide what you're going to have for your next meal while you're preparing your current meal. That will give you time to defrost something if necessary and to double check to make sure you have everything you need.

The Golden Rule of Grocery Shopping

Never, ever go to the grocery store hungry!
You will come home with bags of
munchy food and no real food!

Chapter 11

Money

Over the last seven years of publishing *The Savvy Life*, teaching classes, giving seminars, working one-on-one with clients and through my own personal experiences, I have learned just how strong the emotions around money can be. There is fear about:

- Not having enough money to pay the bills.

- Not knowing how to manage money properly such as balancing bank accounts.

- Attaining wealth only to lose it through poor decision making.

I have also worked with many people who were afraid to even face their finances. They paid their bills erratically and their situation spiraled further out of control.

Like the diet industry, the amount of information on personal finance that is available is inexhaustible. There are many great books out there, but sifting through to find what system works best for you can be overwhelming.

In Chapter 3 - Savvy Habits, we introduced the six habits and routines that help manage your finances effortlessly and successfully. The Savvy Habits are easy to start, easy to maintain and they work. This chapter concentrates on other aspects of personal finance to help you simplify and take control of your money.

In this chapter, we will look at:

- Where your money goes.
- How to organize your finances.
- Different ways to pay your bills.
- Various ways to pay down debt.
- The cash versus debit card question.
- How to really save your money.
- The power of compound interest.
- How to responsibly use credit cards.
- Financial rules of thumb.

Where does all the money go?

Let's say you get paid every other Friday and by the following Thursday, you have $100 left to last for little more than a week. Where does all the money go? It's a truism of engineering that you can't control something until you measure it. That means you can't control your spending until you know <u>how</u> you are spending and <u>on what</u> you are spending.

In 2009, the US Department of Labor did a survey on how the average family's money was spent.

According to the results, the top five expenditures were:

- Housing
- Transportation
- Food
- Insurance and Pensions
- Healthcare

Each individual or family is different. You need to look at your own finances to see where you are spending the most. That is the first place to look for possible ways to save money. It follows the business principle of going after "low-hanging fruit," making the biggest, easiest changes first. But, before you do that exercise, there are some basics to cover first.

Get Organized!

One of the most common reasons people get behind on paying their bills is lack of organization.

- They can't find their bills.

- They don't know when their bills are due.

- They don't know what is automatically coming out of their checking account so money they thought was there, isn't.

- They don't follow Savvy Habit #2 and track their spending on a regular basis. When they do go to pay bills, they have to spend a chunk of time balancing their bank account first or worse, they don't balance their account at all and just hope there's enough money to clear all their bills.

So what can you do to avoid these pitfalls?

Getting organized does not have to involve buying a file cabinet, spending hours labeling file folders and creating complex bill paying processes. In fact, that's exactly what you shouldn't do. Keep the process as simple as possible.

- Use a file folder to keep all of your bills in one place. As bills arrive in the mail, put them directly into your designated folder.

- Within the file folder, organize all the bills by due date.

- Track down your automatic withdrawals and add a print out of the withdrawal statements to your folder.

- Start following Savvy Habit #2 and balance your bank account on a regular basis. Remember, ignorance is expensive.

Now, when payday rolls around, it will be much easier to sit down, pay your bills and enter those transactions into your financial tracking system. It really is that simple. The simpler you keep a process, the greater your chances for maintaining the habit.

Almost every time I've been asked to help a friend streamline their finances, the process of organizing their bills has been the number one task to get them on track. Often, the money to take care of their bills was there, it just wasn't organized in a way they could manage it properly. The beauty of setting up a system like this is you only have to do it once. Then it's a matter of consistently sticking to your organized routine.

Microsoft Money™, Quicken™ or...

There are many good quality financial software products and tracking systems on the market, Microsoft Money™ and Quicken™ from Intuit are two of the best. They both come with lots of bells and whistles including the ability to create reports to see where your money is going.

I have used and enjoyed both products, but in the spirit of simplicity, what has worked best for me - and what I still use - is the straightforward Excel spreadsheet we showed in Chapter 3. It's very similar to a checkbook register, with entries for the check # (when necessary), date, transaction type, transaction number and a running balance.

#	Date	Transaction	Withdrawal	Deposit	Balance	x
	2/15	Salary		1,000.00	1,000.00	x
239	2/15	Safeway Grocery	-75.00		925.00	x

What makes the Excel spreadsheet work so well for me is I use one worksheet per pay period. Instead of a continuous balance, I start a fresh, new worksheet each payday. The worksheets are kept in one Excel workbook document. At the beginning of each year, I start a new workbook.

To balance my account, each morning I open the current spreadsheet and enter my spending for the previous day. I then log into my bank account and check what expenses have cleared, marking an "x" next to those items.

With this process I feel that I have much more control. It offers incentive to stay within my budget and not carry over a negative balance from pay period to pay period. It also feels good to open and close a spreadsheet every two weeks. Most businesses open and close their books quarterly. I happen to do it bi-weekly.

For a free electronic copy of the workbook template visit: www.TheSavvyLife.Com/books/downloads/savvyworkbook.xls.

Whatever system you use, it should be one you find easy and will stick with week after week. It should be easy to see how much money you have right now and what you have been spending your money on.

Paying Your Bills

One of the most important things you can do to control your finances is pay your bills on time. It sounds obvious, but you would be surprised how many people routinely pay bills late. They think, "A few days is no big deal." Actually, it is a big deal. Whether you pay your bills one day late or 29 days late, the fees are the same, and the negative impact on your credit report is the same. Now that you have a system for tracking and organizing your finances, it should be easy to pay your bills on time. What are some of the other ways to stay on top of your bills?

Automatic Withdrawals versus Manual Payments

Every creditor and service provider wants to make it easy for you to give them money. They all have some version of automatic payment that will transfer money from your bank account directly to theirs, without you having to worry about it. This can be good if you're absent-minded, or just don't want to do anything more than keep track of the money going in and out of your pocket. If it makes bill-paying more convenient, you are more likely to stay on top of your bills on a regular basis. It can be bad if you're living close to the edge and don't have enough money in your account to cover the transfer on the day it's scheduled. In that case, you will get hit with <u>both</u> the late fee and the overdraft fee, plus a second fee from your creditor.

My friend Jannette prefers to have her bills automatically paid because it ensures she pays them on time. I prefer to use electronic bill pay through my bank account. Kevin, on the other hand, likes to write checks for all of his bills so he is consciously aware of every expense each month. Every once in awhile think about whether or not your current bill paying system is working for you. If not, consider switching it up. If it's working for you, stick to it!

If you use automatic bill paying, some things to consider are:

- How does the due date mesh with your paycheck deposit?

- Is the bill pay automatically making only the minimum payment each month? This can extend the time it takes you to pay off the debt and will cost you more money in interest.

- What is the creditor's practice regarding weekends and holidays? Will they take the money a day early or a day late?

- If you set up automatic bill pay with a number of creditors, are they all going to be making withdrawals on the same day? Do you regularly have the funds to cover that?

Just because you have automatic bill pay, it doesn't mean you don't have to pay attention to your statements. Companies do make mistakes, so you need to check their statements against your records.

If you pay bills by check, or manual electronic payment:

- Be sure to allow for postage or posting time. Some electronic funds transfers can take up to three days to post to an account.

- Be sure to enclose the payment coupon and write your account number on the check.

- Make sure to use proper postage! Pay attention when the post office changes their rates.

- If you pay by phone, check to make sure there are no additional handling charges.

Payment Due Dates

Every bill you receive has a "pay by this date" notice on it. We have already talked about how important it is to make your payments on time. You need to do this to avoid late fees (typically around $30 - $45), increases in interest rates (up to 40%) and negative comments on your credit report. What if your bills are due the first Thursday of the month and you get paid on the second Friday? If you can't build up a cushion to cover the time difference, contact your creditor and ask them if you can switch your monthly payment due date. Most businesses just want to get paid every month. They don't really care what the actual payment date is.

Do you know you can make more than one payment per month? One of the quickest ways to pay down a debt is to make multiple payments, even if they're small. If you're making electronic payments, it is easy. Just make the payment when you have the extra money. If you're making payments by mail, you need to include a copy of your regular payment stub with all your account information. Just be sure to make your minimum monthly payment on time <u>in addition to any extra payments</u> to avoid confusion or late charges.

Paying Down Your Debts

There are many different philosophies on paying down your debts. All of them have merit. The most important thing is to pick the approach that gives you the greatest satisfaction and keeps you motivated. There are three basic approaches for paying down multiple debts:

- ## Equal Payments

  You can take your available income and divide it by the number of debt accounts you have, making equal payments to each account. If you have determined you have $400 available to pay on your four credit cards and loans, you pay $100 to each one. This is easy to keep track of and manage. You see your balances dropping across the board each month. The drawback to this approach is that you're not considering balance levels or interest rates, so you may end up paying more money than you have to. Make sure the amount you're paying to each account is at least equal to the minimum required payment.

- ## Pay Down the Highest Interest Rate First

  In this approach, you make the minimum payment on all accounts <u>except</u> the one with the highest interest rate. You pay as much as you can on that account until it's paid off, then you tackle the account with the next highest interest rate. You will now be able to make a larger payment, because you can roll in the money you were paying to the now paid off account to that next account. Depending on the relative balances of your accounts, this is usually the best way to minimize the amount of money you pay towards interest.

- ## Pay Off the Lowest Balances First and Compound Your Payments

  In this approach, you make the minimum payments on all accounts <u>except</u> the one with the lowest balance. You pay as much as you can on that account until it's paid off, then you tackle the account with the next lowest balance. It gets easier to pay off each larger balance because you keep rolling in the money from the previously paid off accounts. The advantage to this payment method is that you get concrete, quick feedback. As you pay off each account, you get a large sense of satisfaction. If you get discouraged with seemingly huge amounts of debt, this is a good way to pay it off.

Plug the Leaks

Keep your finances as streamlined as possible and be vigilant about leaks. Automatic withdrawals for things like video subscriptions or gym memberships are something to keep your eye on. Although convenient, if you are not using or benefiting from the programs you signed up for, it is a waste of money. Take a hard look at what is automatically coming out of your account. If you haven't used it in the last few months, spend the five or ten minutes it takes to end the membership. It will pay off. In addition, do whatever it takes to avoid late fees. There are far better was to spend your money than to hand it over because you forgot to return a movie.

Cash versus Debit Card

One of the greatest conveniences of the late 20th century can also be one of the most insidious evils. The debit card has drastically changed the way we conduct personal business. Many people have completely stopped paying with cash, using that little plastic card for buying everything from coffee and donuts to furniture and small appliances. There are some very good reasons for using a debit card instead of cash. You don't need to worry about carrying large amounts of cash, or going to the bank before running errands. You don't have to worry about the cashier giving you the correct change, or figuring out what to do with all those loose coins. You get a record of every single purchase you make.

However, there is a dark side to using debit cards. Most people will think before using a credit card because they don't want to pay the interest unless they absolutely have to. Additionally, many businesses will not accept credit cards for small purchases. Everybody takes debit cards, and there doesn't seem to be any downsides to paying with them instead of cash. The big problem with using debit cards instead of cash is most people do not consciously realize they are spending money when they use a debit card. When you pull out five crisp $20 dollar bills and hand them over, you are intimately aware of the fact that you just surrendered your hard-earned money. When you give the merchant your magic money card and he just swipes it, the emotional attachment is not there.

The psychological difference of automatic payments versus cash is evident with toll transponders. Many municipalities have figured out if commuters have to reach into their wallets for the cash to pay a toll each time they cross a bridge or go on a toll road, they are very sensitive to toll increases and will complain about it for months. If the commuters are using electronic payment transponders, they quickly forget about the toll increases because the tolls are automatically deducted from an escrow account on a monthly basis. They don't get that painful daily reminder of handing over the extra fifty cents or dollar bill.

If you make a practice of paying for discretionary purchases with cash instead of a debit card, you will find yourself acutely aware of every purchase. That simple shift in behavior will give you the few seconds to ask yourself "is this purchase really worth the money I am going to spend?" Try it for thirty days and see if you become more aware of how you spend your money.

Let's Make a Deal

Speaking of being aware of how you spend your money, it's so important that you pay attention to all of your expenditures. At least once a quarter, review your bills and if necessary, see where you can save. Call your credit card companies to see if you can get a lower rate. Call your cable and telephone companies to see if they are offering any deals. Most of these companies know it takes much less energy to keep a current customer than to get a new one. Often, you can get a deal just by asking. You don't even have to threaten to change vendors. However, it always pays to do a little research before you call. If you can tell the representative that you *know* you can get a better deal at his competitor because you just checked, it makes your bargaining position that much stronger. It may not seem like a lot at first, but it adds up! Just be sure you read the fine print before you make any changes. Introductory and teaser offers are great, as long as you don't find yourself locked into a long-term contract with changing rates after that low introductory period.

Play Hard to Get

In the previous chapters it was suggested that you set up spending accounts to help you save for your financial goals such as a vacations or hobbies. Remember, these are spending accounts as they are short term savings with the intention of spending.

An emergency savings account is for saving in case of emergency. An emergency is a job loss or an unexpected car repair. You don't want to put the expense on your credit card. A savings account that you tap into on a regular basis is not a savings account. It's a holding account!

Put your savings where it's accessible in an emergency, but a little hard to get. If it's not linked to your ATM you won't have the ability to tap into it at a weak moment. Also, set up rules around the account and decide in advance what equates to an "emergency". If this is a real weakness for you, ask a trusted friend to be your judge. Tell them in advance what your rules are around the account. When trying to decide if you should withdraw from the account, call your friend and let them judge, based on your rules, if your situation is actually an emergency.

The Power of Compound Interest

Compound interest means that interest is paid not only on the principal (initial balance), but also on the interest it earns. It's phenomenal if you are on the receiving end. It's devastating if you are on the paying end.

*"The most powerful force in the universe
is compound interest."*

— Albert Einstein

The Power of Compound Interest - for Good

Suppose you get a $2,000 tax refund one year and put it in a CD account yielding 4%. In one year, you will make $80 interest. In 12 years, you might expect to make $960 ($80 X 12). In fact, you will make just over $1200 in interest (maybe more, depending on how frequently your bank compounds the interest). In 18 years, you will double your money, <u>with no further contribution on your part</u>.

The Power of Compound Interest - for Evil

Now let's look at what happens when you are on the "giving" end. Suppose you have a credit card with $5,000 debt, at a 12% interest rate. Every month you make the minimum payment, which starts at $125 and drops down as you pay off the card. If you never charge another dollar on this credit card, it will take you over 18 years to pay it off, at which point, you will have paid a total of $8,180 on that $5,000 debt.

If you pay a steady $125 until you pay it off, you can pay off that same $5,000 in a little over 4 years, at a total cost of $6,400. Why the savings? Because the credit card issuers compound your debt every month (or in some cases, every day). That means every month, they calculate the interest on your outstanding balance and add it to the total you owe. The longer you take to pay off the debt, the more times they get to add that interest to the balance.

The figure below shows the effect of compound interest on debts and savings. The solid line shows the payoff of a $5,000 credit line, making the minimum payment each month. The dotted line shows the payoff for the same $5,000, making a fixed $125 payment each month. The dot-dash line shows the gain investment for a $2,000 savings deposit paying 4% annual interest.

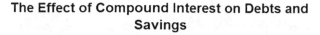

The Effect of Compound Interest on Debts and Savings

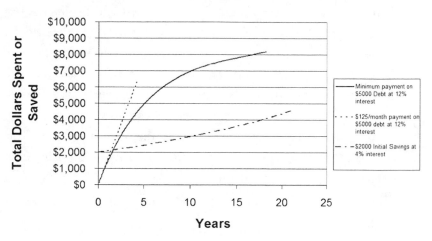

Use the power of compound interest to your benefit. The more you save, the more it grows. Conversely the quicker you pay off debts, the less money in interest you pay.

Are Credit Cards Pure Evil?

There are some financial advisors who say you should pay off your credit cards and cut them up, never to use them again. You don't have to be quite so extreme. Most tools are useful when used properly, in moderation. So, how can you safely use credit cards?

1. Treat them as an extension of your cash, not as fairy godmothers.

    Establish a budget for yourself. Whether you pay with cash or credit, if you spend within your means, you will be better off. Determine how much money you can spend in a month and stick to it.

2. Pay them off in a reasonable amount of time.

If you do pay your credit cards off every month, you minimize your interest payments. (Some card issuers give you a 20-day interest-free grace period. Others start charging you interest from the day you make your purchase.) However, if you set up your budget to make a credit card purchase and pay it off within 3 months, and you stick to that budget, you will be responsibly using your available funds. The key is to determine what the total cost to you will be <u>before</u> you make the purchase. This includes the purchase price and the accrued interest charges. You then have to determine if it is within your budget and if it is worth that total cost.

3. Only use them when they really are the best alternative.

If you cannot afford to pay cash for something, consider why. Also, consider why you need to make the purchase now instead of saving up for it and whether there are any other options. Does the store have a layaway policy?

When does it make sense to buy on credit instead of waiting until you have saved the money to purchase it outright?

• If the item is on sale for a significant savings now and won't be when you have the cash. Be sure to include the cost of interest in determining if the sale price is good enough to justify the credit purchase.

• If waiting will cost you more money. For instance, if you have a leaky dishwasher or refrigerator that cannot be repaired and waiting until you have the cash to purchase a new one will result in increased water damage to your floor. In that case, it may make sense to buy the replacement appliance on credit.

• If you need the protection provided by credit card purchases. Most credit card issuers offer some type of buyer protection where they will cancel a charge <u>after</u> a dispute has been settled.

Note that you still have to make payments while the case is being investigated. But, if the investigation is decided in your favor, the credit card company will refund your account for the charge. This can be easier than trying to collect money from the vendor yourself. Each credit card company handles this slightly differently, so be sure to read your card agreement carefully to understand how yours works.

4. Set up rules and abide by them.

By setting up boundaries around how you use your credit cards, you will keep their use in check. Some suggestions include:

- Limit yourself to one major credit card with a credit limit you can handle.

- Do not use the card a second time until you have paid off the previous balance.

- Always make the payments before the due date. This ensures you don't incur a late fee, but it also positively affects your credit score. Pay late and your credit score will be negatively impacted, affecting your ability to get a loan in the future when you may really need it.

If you view credit purchases as a "court of last resort," only using them when you absolutely have to and honestly calculate the total cost of using them, you will be using them responsibly.

If you have continuously struggled with credit card debt in the past and you know it is a weakness for you, staying away from them altogether is your best alternative.

Financial Rules of Thumb

Making major financial decisions can be difficult. The fear of making a mistake and the long term consequences make it difficult to move forward.

Recognized financial expert Gregory Karp published an excellent set of financial rules of thumb in The Morning Call in 2010. With his permission, we are pleased to reprint excerpts from that article:

Abide by Financial Rules of Thumb to Prosper
By Gregory Karp
The Morning Call *(Allentown, Pa.) (MCT)*

Money rules of thumb can be inaccurate because people's financial lives differ so much. But they can help us make difficult decisions or give us benchmarks. Here are a few:

- **Rule of 10:** For perspective on big purchases, think about how you will feel about it in 10 days, 10 weeks and 10 years. For a luxury car: In 10 days, I'll still be excited about the new-car smell and its nice ride. In 10 weeks, it's just the machine I use to get to work and the supermarket. In 10 years, I'll barely remember this car.

- **House payment:** Your mortgage, including taxes and insurance, should not exceed 29 percent of your gross monthly income.

- **Car payment:** All vehicle payments should not exceed 15 percent of your take-home pay.

- **Total debt:** Total monthly debt payments should not exceed 36 percent of your gross monthly income.

- **Car repair:** If the auto repair costs less than half of the trade-in value, repair it. Otherwise, consider selling it and buying another.

- **Holiday gifts:** Spend no more than 1.5 percent of your gross income on the holidays, including gifts and travel.

- **Restaurant tipping:** To quickly figure a generous tip, double the first digit on your bill. For bills more than $100, double the first two digits.

- **Emergency fund:** Keep a rainy-day fund equal to three to six months of expenses.

- **Debt payment:** Pay debts from highest interest rate to lowest. Or from the smallest amount to largest.

- **College borrowing:** Don't borrow more money than you'll make in your first year working after graduation.

- **Choose experiences:** In a choice between spending on things or experiences with other people, choose the latter. Research shows it makes us happier.

- Never:
  - ◊ Lend money to friends and family.
  - ◊ Borrow from your 401(k) or cash out early.
  - ◊ Pay fees on a checking account.
  - ◊ Buy an extended warranty.
  - ◊ Buy an investment you don't understand.

This chapter includes some of mine and Kevin's favorite money management tips that we either employ ourselves or have successfully worked for our family and friends. However you choose to handle your finances, keep it as simple as possible. Create your system and stick to it. Your goal is to manage your money instead of allowing it to manage you.

Top 10 Tips for Money

---

1. Create a pleasant space in your house for paying your bills and managing your money. Make it as inviting as possible so you actually want to spend time there.

2. When donating items to thrift stores, grab a receipt to deduct those items from your taxes.

3. Consider using cash as your "fun" money. Use it for dining out, admission to movies or buying "toys". When your cash is used up for that pay period, you will have to wait until the following pay period

to replenish. Keeping your fun money separate from your regular "living" money can help keep you from overspending.

4. Be respectful of your money. Keep your wallet neat and organized.

5. Continue your education. Take classes to learn about investing and retirement strategies.

6. Start reading at least two financial magazines per month.

7. Your attitude about managing your finances will directly impact your willingness to do it. Get excited that you are taking control of your finances and keep in mind all the different ways it will positively impact your entire life.

8. Find a mentor. If you know someone who lives the savvy life, pick their brain!

9. Remember to keep your finances as simple as possible. By staying on top of your routine, it should take you no more than 20 minutes each pay period to pay your bills and get a snapshot of your current financial status.

10. Don't be embarrassed about the state of your finances. That can be paralyzing. If you aren't happy where you stand financially, take action! Start by getting yourself organized and create a plan of attack. Even if you have to take it in baby steps, you will be moving toward your goal.

Chapter 12

What is Important to You?

Living the Savvy Life is about choices. It's about saving on the things that aren't as important to you so you can afford to spend money on the things that are important to you.

You may have a general idea of what is important to you. You might have goals that you want to focus your spending on such as a house, a dream vacation, or something as simple as updating your wardrobe. As you have already learned, defining those goals and writing them down will help you achieve them faster. But have you ever sat down and looked at your life as a whole and how you want to live it - then planned your spending to achieve it?

This type of thought and planning allows you to live a more purposeful life. Instead of going where the wind takes you, you have control and can direct your life according to where you want to go. Of course you want to be flexible and leave room for serendipitous moments, but having a design in mind for what you want your life to be like and how to achieve it is powerful.

My friend Jessica, whom I talked about in the wardrobe chapter, is an excellent example of a designer of her own life. From the way she dresses to where she lives and what she does in her free time, she makes conscious decisions to get herself there. She decides what's important enough to spend her money on and where she should focus her savings.

My savvy friend Carla A. is also very purposeful with her life. From where she works, what she buys and where she vacations, it's done with intent.

Everyone is different and has different dreams. There is no one-size-fits-all answer and that is a wonderful thing. Your life is yours to create and do with as you will. We have designed a questionnaire to help you evaluate your current life and to craft goals based on where you are now and where you want to be in the near future.

Begin with the End in Mind

A powerful way to achieve the life you want is to start by thinking big - your ultimate goals. The first series of questions focuses on the idea that money is no object. Often, without meaning to, we put limitations on our dreams. Take this part seriously and think honestly about the life you want to live if money is no object.

From there, you can go through the remaining questions. You may realize that you are happier in your current life than you originally thought. Or you may decide that you want to make some serious changes. Regardless, these first questions will get you thinking. Be willing to dream big!

- If money was no object, what would your lifestyle be like?
- Where would you live?
- Where would you vacation?
- Where and what would you eat?
- What clothes would you wear?
- Where would you work?
- How many hours per day would you work?
- What would you do with your non-working time?
- Where do you want to be in ten years?

Now that you are in a mindset without limits it's time to go through the areas of your life that we touched on in the last six chapters.

Home

- Are you happy where you live?
- What makes you happy about your home?
- What are your frustrations with your home?
- What would you like your house to look like in one year?
- Do you have any "ultimate goals" for your home?
- What can you do right now to make your home more enjoyable?
- Do you want to move? If so, where do you want to move to?

Entertainment

- What do you enjoy doing in your free time?
- How much time do you spend doing the things you want to do?
- What is your ideal way to spend an afternoon?
- What is your ideal way to spend a weekend?
- If you aren't spending your weekends as you would like, why not?
- What are you not doing now that you really want to do? Why not?
- When you are with friends, what do you usually do and do you enjoy those activities?
- Where would you like to vacation within the next year?
- What is your ideal way to spend an extended vacation?
- Do you have any ultimate travel or leisure goals?

Wardrobe and Beauty

- Do you dress the way you would like?
- Does your hair, skin and makeup look the way you would like?
- Are you happy with the way you present yourself?
- Of the clothes currently in your closet, what percentage do you wear on a regular basis?
- What frustrates you about your wardrobe?

- What frustrates you about your hair and makeup?
- Is there a celebrity you would like to dress similarly to? If so, what is it about their style that you like?
- If you had a wardrobe, hair and makeup stylist, what would you tell them?
- If you could go to a spa on a regular basis, what treatments would you get?
- Do you have any ultimate goals regarding your appearance?

Food

- Do you cook at home?
- Do you enjoy cooking?
- How often do you dine out?
- Where do you eat out?
- Where would you like to eat out?
- If you don't enjoy cooking, why not?
- Do you want to improve your cooking skills? If so, how do you want to do it? Take classes or learn from a family member?
- Do you like eating? Is it a pleasurable experience to be savored and dwelt on, or is it a necessity to keep your body functioning?
- If you had a personal live-in chef, what would you have him or her cook for each meal?
- Are you happy with your dining habits? For example: do you sit at a table and enjoy your food or do you eat as quickly as possible while driving to your next commitment?
- If you are unhappy with your dining habits, what can you do immediately to change them?
- Do you have any ultimate goals regarding cooking and dining?

The following questions dig a little deeper to help you hone your money savvy skills.

Money

- Do you keep track of your spending?
- Do you have a process and routine for paying bills?
- If placed on the spot, could you say how much you earn and how much you owe?
- Do you spend less than you make?
- Are you putting money into an emergency savings and retirement account on a regular basis?
- Do you like making money or is it just a necessary evil?
- Do you enjoy your job? If not, what would you prefer to be doing? What can you do to make that happen?
- Do you like getting bargains or do you just want to buy what you need and be done with it?
- What is your financial goal for one year from now?
- What is your ultimate financial goal?

Evaluate - Plan - Implement

Now that you have completed the questionnaire it is time to assess your current status and craft a plan to create the life you want. The following steps will guide you.

1. Go back and review your answers.

2. Evaluate where you are happy and where you are frustrated.

3. Look for simple ways to improve your lifestyle immediately and implement them.

4. Look for areas that you want to improve, but need more time, money or effort to do it.

5. Define those longer term goals and create small steps to move you toward them.

6. Create a personal deadline for each step and make it happen!

Each time you answer a question with "I can't do that," stop and answer the question "Why not?" Do this seven times. By the seventh time, you should be able to identify the true roadblock and come up with a way to either achieve your goal or redefine it into something more manageable.

Although it may take time, this exercise is one of the most powerful tools to put you on the path to living the life you want. If you have not answered the questionnaire yet, STOP READING! Go back and take the time to really think about your life and what is important to you. For a free electronic copy of the questionnaire visit:

www.TheSavvyLife.Com/books/downloads/savvyquestionnaire.pdf

If you have decided to make a lot of changes to your life, it can be overwhelming. This can lead to frustration, making you decide to throw away your plan altogether. In the fitness and nutrition world, we call this "screw it" mode. Don't go into "screw it" mode! You have the power to achieve your goals!

In the school where I learned kung fu, there was a famous saying printed on the wall that has defined the way I look at goals:

"A journey of a thousand miles begins with a single step."

— Lao-Tzu

- One step at a time, I got through my first kung fu class.
- One step at a time, I earned my first belt.
- One step at a time I fought my first sparring match.
- One step at a time I earned my first black belt.
- One step at a time I earned my second black belt.
- One step at a time I am working toward my third black belt.

This same philosophy applies to everything. Break down your goal into smaller pieces and take it one step at a time.

Make it a habit to review your answers to the questionnaire every three months. The change of the season is a fitting time to do it. Read through your answers and see how you have progressed. Congratulate yourself on the goals you have accomplished.

Of those you have yet to accomplish, take some time to think about why you haven't been able to make it happen. You may need to break those particular goals down into even smaller, bite-sized pieces. For example, if your goal is to enhance your quality of life by eating all of your meals at the dinner table, you may want to start by deciding to eat at least two meals a week at the table. Once you have been able to do that for a few weeks, increase your goal to three nights a week and so on.

As you grow, your goals will evolve. You will have achieved many of your aspirations and with that, your perspective will shift. Over time, be willing to amend your answers so they fall in line with your current aspirations. This type of growth is the sign of living with purpose.

Congratulations - you are now the designer of your life!

Chapter 13

Savvy
Shopping

Savvy shopping isn't just about getting a good price on an item. It's about picking and choosing what you want to spend your money on. It's about planning, forethought and anticipation. It's about being willing to "sleep on it" and about returning items that don't work for you.

Savvy shopping is a skill. It takes time, but it can be learned and mastered. Here is where the Savvy Life Philosophy really comes into play: Save money on the things that aren't important to you so you can spend money on the things that are important to you.

The following tools, habits and ideas will help you achieve more successful shopping adventures.

Spending Book

In Chapter 6, we introduced the idea of a spending book. This is a small notebook you keep with you at all times. In it, you list the items you want to purchase that are outside of your normal household spending (i.e. groceries). In your spending book you can list the specific clothes you want to add to your wardrobe. You can keep a list of the books and movies you want to buy. You can include the towels you need to purchase or the lamp you want to get for your bedroom.

The idea of the spending book is to use it as a tool to focus your discretionary income on what you truly want. By adding an item to the book, you are creating an intention. You have decided that item is important enough to spend your money on. Soon, it will become your habit to walk into a store and only purchase items that are on your list (i.e. grocery) or in your spending book. However, remember to be open to serendipity. If you walk into a store and absolutely fall in love with an item that is not on your list and you know it is true love, be willing to purchase it as long as it is within your spending budget at that time. If not, add it to your spending book and start saving for it.

Some of the items on your wish list may not be achievable immediately. That's OK. By having them on your list, it will keep reminding you to look for ways to save in other areas so you can focus the saved money on that bigger ticket item.

As you go through your favorite store's weekly sales ads, consult your spending book to see if any of the items you want happen to be on sale. After we remodeled our home, I had a rather long list of items to purchase in my spending book. Each week, I would go through the sales ads of my favorite stores and look for the items that were on my list. If it was a good enough sale, I would go out and purchase the item. By being patient and timing my purchases I was able to save 20 - 50% on the items I needed and wanted.

The habit of reading through your spending book before walking into a store will help keep you focused. It's so easy to get distracted. Stores spend millions of dollars on marketing and displays to get you to spend. Make sure you are spending on what you truly want. Your spending book will help you.

Fall in Love

Only purchase things you love. You will be amazed at how much this simple practice will modify what you bring into your home and how much money it will save you. By only purchasing things you love, you will be able to afford those items, even if they are more expensive than what you normally spend, because you are no longer throwing your money at items that aren't worthy of bringing home.

Before heading to the checkout stand, take a look at your intended purchases and start editing. Of each item, ask yourself:

- Do I need it?

- Will I really use it?

- Do I love it?

If the answer is no, then put the item back. If you are at the register and your gut tells you not to purchase the item, tell the clerk you changed your mind and don't want it. There is no shame in that. In fact, it's empowering. You have taken control of what you are purchasing and bringing into your home. Congratulations!

You can incorporate this same habit at the grocery store. Look at your cart for impulse items and ask yourself if you really want to make those purchases. Impulse items such as flavored drinks and snacks can increase your grocery bill by 20% or more.

One other tactic is to sleep on it. Wait at least 24 hours before making the purchase. If you are still thinking about it the next day, then it is most likely worth purchasing.

Plan, Plan, Plan!

Planning is another powerful tool for savvy shopping. How often have you had to spend more than you wanted on a gift because you waited until the last minute to go shopping? Worse, how often have you paid more for a gift you weren't that excited about giving, because you didn't allow yourself enough time to find the perfect item? A little forethought and planning gives you control over your non-routine purchases and helps reduce those surprise expenditures.

Planning also allows you to enjoy anticipation. It allows you to search for and find exactly what you want and need. Planning allows you to research the best price or sit back and see if the item goes on sale. It allows you to save up so you can purchase exactly what you want instead of settling for what you can afford at the moment. Waiting until the last minute can lead to overspending and having to settle for less than you want.

At the beginning of each month take a look at your calendar for that month and the following one. Are there any events that require a purchase of some sort?

- Do you need a new comforter for the coming winter months?
- Do you need a dress for your cousin's wedding?
- Do you need a bathing suit for your vacation to Hawaii?

If so, start shopping now! It's a simple, yet powerful habit to adopt. Don't wait until the last minute. Remember, this type of planning allows you the time you need to find what you want and often at the price you want to pay. It also greatly reduces the stress associated with trying to find what you need at the last minute.

Gift Giving

Like social spending, gift giving can be one of the greatest budget busters. Planning is your greatest ally. Check your calendar at least two months in advance for any upcoming events such as weddings, birthdays and holidays. Add the recipient's name to your spending book and it will help you remember to keep an eye out for gifts.

By planning in advance you can watch for sales. Even better, you can stumble upon the "perfect" gift rather than settle for something less.

Important: With all of your planning you will have the opportunity to save a lot of money on gifts. Do not fall into the trap of, "I only spent $5 on that book for my brother. I should get him something else too." Your brother doesn't know you only spent $5 on that beautiful book for him. Remember, gift giving should have nothing to do with the amount you spend. It's the thought and intention behind the gift that counts.

Invest or Bargain Shop?

Shopping requires constant decision making. One of the major decisions to be made is whether to invest in an item or to bargain shop. This is a personal decision, as the things that are important to you and worth an investment may not be important to the next person.

What do I invest in?

- Wardrobe Classics - I'm willing to spend more money on classic wardrobe pieces, because I know I will wear them on a regular basis. Also, because they are not trendy items, I will be able to keep them in circulation for years. I want to make sure they last.

- Furniture - I'm willing to spend more on furniture because I'm going to sit on it, sleep on it or use it every day. I want to ensure the items are good quality and last as long as possible. Also, because I'm going to use them every day for years, I want to make sure I purchase what I really want and not settle for something I may not love, just because it's cheaper.

- Vacations - I'm willing to spend more on vacations because they are often once-in-a-lifetime experiences and I want to enjoy myself. I will also spend more in this area because vacations are very important to me and my family.

Just because I am willing to invest in the above items, doesn't mean I still won't look for the best price or wait for a good sale.

What do I bargain shop for?

- Trendy Clothes - It's rare that I purchase trendy clothes, but if there is something I like, I will try to find it at the best possible price. I know I will only be able to wear it for a few months so I strive to reduce my price per wear as much as possible.

- Groceries - I'm willing to invest in quality food, but I am able to bargain shop for much of what I bring home. If I purchase packaged foods, I look for the best possible price. Also, as discussed in Chapter 10, I plan our meals based on what is on sale for that week. Food really is one of the easiest areas of your life to save money.

- Books and Movies - Books are an important commodity in our household and we are willing to invest in them. If I really want or need a book and I know it won't be on sale for awhile, I go ahead and pay full price. If it is something that I don't need immediately, I'll add the title to my spending book and look for it on PaperBackSwap. com, Half.com or when I go to the used book store. I go through the same process with movies we want to add to our video library.

A loose guideline is to invest in things that need to last more than a few years or have sentimental value.

A final note about investing and bargain shopping: buy what you want, not what you can afford at the moment. Be willing to wait for it. Don't settle for a cheaper item just because you aren't willing to save for what you really want. Often, in the long run, it's more expensive to purchase the cheaper item - because it's inferior or because you won't have the satisfaction the more expensive item would give you. Without that satisfaction, you will likely end up purchasing the more expensive item on top of the cheaper one, costing you far more in the long run.

Let the Stores Help You

As a result of the recession in 2008, many stores brought back layaway service. Stores such as Sears, Kmart, Burlington Coat Factory and Marshalls will allow you to put a deposit down on an item and then pay for it in installments over the course of 4 - 8 weeks. The deposits and service fees vary from store to store. What I like about layaway programs is that it's like a reverse credit card system. Using an installment method, you pay for your purchase in advance.

Your spending book is an excellent planning tool. The Internet is another. Sign up for your favorite store's mailing list. You will be notified of sales and sent coupons! You may also be informed of special sales not available to the public.

My friend Alison Gary who writes her own blog, WardrobeOxygen.com, is a huge fan of Ebates, the online cash back shopping site. Membership to Ebates is free. The company pays members 1% - 20% cash back every time they shop online as well as providing them with coupons and online deals.

Visit the Ebates site, search for your favorite online retailer, and click on their site through the link provided by Ebates. Then four times a year, Ebates will send you a check in the mail.

Alison recently posted, "No contracts, no giving all your personal information, no strings attached. Last year I made over $700 for just shopping for the regular purchases I make. I don't need a taskbar, I don't need to collect points, I don't have to scour the Internet for codes, I don't need to buy from shops I don't know or regularly frequent." Alison is a very savvy woman!

It's interesting to note that Ebates was founded in 1998 by two Deputy District Attorneys in Silicon Valley who used to prosecute online fraud and identity theft before starting the online company.

Returns

Don't be afraid to return an item. As a consumer, you have the right to return a purchase as long as you follow the store's return policy. Just make sure you return it. It is worth taking the five to ten minutes to get your money back or exchange the item for what you really want.

If you have a pile of clothes in your closet with the tags still on, then you need to change the way you shop. If you aren't good at returning purchases and you have any question that an item may not work out for you - leave it at the store.

The Power of Anticipation

When was the last time you got excited about a purchase? When was the last time you bought something and it really made you happy for hours, days or even weeks?

As adults, we have the ability to buy what we want, when we want, whether we can afford it or not. A sad byproduct of this type of consumerism is the lack of anticipation. You no longer look forward to making a purchase. You often just buy it on credit. Instead of the joys of anticipation, you experience the dread of your credit card bill.

Even if you can afford an item right away, consider waiting before making the purchase. Anticipating an item gives you time to think about it. If you wait a day or a week and you are still thinking about it, chances are it will continue to make you happy. If a day or a week later you have forgotten about it, then you have saved money and clutter! This is an easy and useful tool to ensure you fill your home only with things that you love.

Using anticipation as a way to curb impulse purchases is an enjoyable way to control a harmful habit. Impulse purchases steal your focus from the financial goals you have set, whether it is a vacation to France or achieving a certain amount in your emergency savings account. Using anticipation will help keep you focused to spend the money on the things you want.

Waiting to purchase an item adds to its emotional value. You will appreciate the item you waited for so much more than anything purchased on a whim.

Pay Attention to Your Environment

As mentioned earlier, advertisers invest millions of dollars to figure out how to get people to buy. Some tricks are as subtle as fast food restaurants blowing their kitchen exhaust out at street level to make those who pass by hungry. Don't hold it against them for trying. It's their job. Just be aware of what they are doing. When you see something you want to buy, take the time to look around you and determine if you want to buy it because of where you are and what you see. This is especially important when you are on vacation or attending fairs and festivals. That cute bodice and peasant blouse may look like a great deal in the Renaissance Festival "shoppe," but not so much when you get home and realize there is absolutely no other place you would wear it.

It's a Process

As we said at the start of this chapter, savvy shopping is a skill. It takes time, but it can be learned and mastered. Watch for signs that tell you how you're doing. If you went clothes shopping last weekend and the bags are still sitting on your couch untouched, you're probably not in love with what you purchased. If you were, you would have immediately come home and hung them in your closet or have already worn them. Keep at it. Little by little you will be the savviest of shoppers.

Chapter 14

Celebrity Savvy
Life Role Models

Throughout this book, we have told you inspirational stories of men and women who have taught us lessons on savvy living. Read on to learn about celebrities who are living the savvy life on a grander scale. They understand the Savvy Life Philosophy and the Golden Rule. They are wealthy enough to buy whatever they want, with just a little concern for budgeting, yet they choose to live prudently. They save on the things that aren't important to them and spend on the things that are important to them.

Rachael Ray
Television Star

Despite her own success Rachael Ray's work encourages a savvy lifestyle. Her show *30 Minute Meals* on the Food Network shows you how to prepare delicious meals at home with ingredients that aren't overly complicated or expensive.

Her travel show *$40 a Day* shows you where to go to enjoy three meals and a snack during your travels to some of the most cosmopolitan cities in the world for - $40 a day.

Unlike many women who achieve financial success, Rachael Ray remembers what it was like to have to work hard just to make ends meet. She even hosted a segment titled "Bang for your Buck" on her popular talk show *Rachael Ray*.

In a June 6, 2008 interview with Bankrate.com, *"Fame & Fortune: Rachael Ray"*, she talked about how much of her spending habits are the same as before she was famous. "But in our everyday life, I wear literally the same pants I've had for 10, 12 years. I still shop at T.J. Maxx and Marshalls and Target, and I do my own grocery shopping." Rachael goes on to say, "So my everyday life is very much the same. But we can afford to share a lot with our family in ways we couldn't afford to do before, and we can do great fun things that are emotionally profitable for us, like starting the Yum-O! organization."

Sarah Michelle Gellar
Movie and Television Star

Growing up in a single parent household, Sarah Michelle Gellar gained an appreciation for savvy money management. Although she enjoys a successful movie and television career, she is still mindful of her spending. In a 2007 interview with *Self* magazine, Sarah stated, "I take my reusable bag to Whole Foods so I get a discount. I go to Bloomingdale's on double reward days. And I always print my dry cleaning coupons before I go."

Sophia Loren
International Movie Star

Sophia Loren didn't start out the glamorous icon that she is today. She was born an illegitimate child in Italy and grew up poverty stricken and malnourished. Day-to-day life was extremely difficult for the young girl. After getting a start in beauty pageants she became an international sensation as a skilled and talented actress. Through acting she became independently wealthy, but has held on to her down-to-earth persona. She continues to balance the lavishness of celebrity with the simplicity of her life at home in Switzerland, including cooking for her family. She focuses her time and her money on what is truly important to her.

Halle Berry

Actor

Halle Berry is a rarity in the celebrity world. Despite making millions of dollars per movie, she is careful with her spending. She has the insight to understand the unpredictability of her industry and saves accordingly. She has been quoted as saying that she doesn't have 10 cars or spend money on diamonds. A secure financial future is more important to her than the trappings of many of her celebrity counterparts.

Teri Hatcher

Actor

Teri Hatcher has had a long career that truly exploded with the success of Desperate Housewives. Yet, she continues to maintain a savvy lifestyle.

In a 2005 interview, she told *People* magazine, "I don't spend my money on sports cars or new million-dollar houses, but being able to go on the trip of a lifetime is pretty special. I'm a very conservative person. I drive my cars for 10 years until they have 100,000 miles on them. To me, feeling comfortable means having way more than I need in the bank."

The media is littered with horror stories of the famous who lose everything by spending more than they make. It's nice to know there are celebrities out there who respect their own hard work enough to be savvy with their money.

Chapter 15

The Core of
the Savvy Life

The beauty of *Living the Savvy Life* is that the foundation of it requires just one rule, a philosophy and six habits. This chapter summarizes and reinforces the core of the savvy lifestyle.

One Rule

The Golden Rule, and the only way to achieve financial success, is to spend less than you make. Directing money into some type of retirement and emergency savings account is the key to following the Golden Rule effortlessly.

- Set your ultimate savings goal - we suggest 20% of your income achieved over the course of time - 15% in a retirement account and 5% in an emergency savings account.

- Underachieve - start with a small savings target and slowly work your way up to your ultimate goal. It's ok if it takes several years to get to that 20% goal.

- Save it! Place your emergency savings in an account that is not easily accessible and define ahead of time what is a real emergency.

One Philosophy

The Savvy Life Philosophy is to save money on the things that aren't important to you so you can afford to spend money on the things that are important to you.

Incorporate this into your thought process. With each purchase, whether it's clothes or groceries, decide on the importance of the item to you and whether you want to spend your money or save it.

Be flexible. If fashion is one of the most important things to you, that doesn't mean you have to spend every dime on fashion and be overly frugal every where else. More than likely, you will save and spend on various items within each area.

The Savvy Life Philosophy is all about making your dollar count and spending it on the things that give you pleasure and make you happy versus meaninglessly consuming.

Six Habits

Habits and routines allow you to manage your finances successfully. To review, the six Savvy Habits are:

- Pay yourself first. Have money automatically taken out of your paycheck and put into your retirement and emergency savings account. This is the habit that makes it easy to spend less than you make.

- Track your spending. The only way to truly know where you stand financially is to track your spending and regularly balance your account. Make it a habit to balance it first thing every morning. When balanced regularly, it will take just a few minutes and you will know exactly where you stand.

- Pay all of your bills on payday. Paying your bills on payday ensures the money is available. Payday is also a great time to fill your gas tank and buy groceries. Now you know exactly how much discretionary income you have for that pay period to spend as you please.

- <u>Set financial goals.</u> Whether it's a house, a vacation or a new car, define and set your goals. This process will help you focus and attain your goals far faster than simply wishing for them. It's much easier to realize your dreams once they are clearly defined.

- <u>Know when to invest and when to bargain shop</u>. Before making a purchase, think about what you need it for and how long you want it to last. Then decide if it's time to invest or bargain shop.

- <u>Spend money on the things you want.</u> A key habit for the savvy person happens as you approach the check out register. Scan your basket and make sure the items in there are the things you intended on purchasing in the first place and you really want. If any stowaways jumped in your basket, turn around and put them back. Stay focused and only spend money on the things you really want.

One rule, a philosophy and six habits is all it takes to adopt the savvy lifestyle and thrive. Within weeks, if not days, they will be routine and effortless.

Chapter 16

Tricks to Stay Motivated

Going back to the diet analogy, staying motivated is the hardest part of any lifestyle change. The good news is that after a very short time, the philosophy, habits and routines presented in this book will become second nature. Also, as you start seeing small successes, it will inspire you toward your ultimate savvy goals. In the meantime, we have a few suggestions to keep you motivated.

Keep Your Eye on the Prize

Most of us are much more successful when there is a motivating goal involved. Being able to lose that last five pounds for your wedding is a perfect example.

Do you have a goal that you have been trying to achieve? Let's say you want to take a trip to Italy. It's something you have dreamed about for years, but you haven't been able to make it materialize. You can make it happen.

Start researching your trip immediately:

- Decide what time of year you want to go, where you want to visit and how long you want to stay.

- Investigate the cost of flights, hotel and ground transportation.

- Do as much research as possible to give you a very clear idea of what is involved.

The next step is to give yourself visual reminders to keep you focused. Start by putting notes with the word "Italy" on your credit and debit cards. Every time you pull that card out to make a purchase, you will have a reminder of your ultimate goal. Through this process, you will start getting a lot more picky about how you use those cards.

Next, find a few pictures of where you want to go in Italy and tape it next to your computer and on your refrigerator. Put them where you will see them on a regular basis. Pictures are highly motivating.

Finally, as we previously advised, set up that spending account specifically for this trip. An account dedicated to that vacation will ensure the money doesn't accidentally get absorbed elsewhere. Start shoveling money into this account whenever possible. With the proper motivation, you will be amazed at all the different places you can find extra money for your goals.

One other tip - set a goal date. "I want to go on my trip to Italy on July 15, 2015." With a defined goal date, you will have much more success in obtaining it. Without a time frame, the goal will always be a trip you want to take in the future.

Your Net Worth

Keeping track of your net worth is another highly motivating tool. Your net worth is the total of your assets (everything you own outright) calculated against your debts.

This number is more motivating because it moves fast. It contains the entire picture of your assets and liabilities, accurately reflecting your financial status. The higher your net worth, the more freedom you will have to do what you want.

To calculate your net worth:

- **Step 1:** List all of your fixed assets, such as real estate and cars at their current value.

- **Step 2:** List all of your liquid assets: cash, CDs, stocks, bonds, retirement account, emergency savings and all other bank accounts.

- **Step 3:** List all jewelry, furniture and household items at their current value.

- **Step 4:** Add together all of the above. These are your total assets.

- **Step 5:** Subtract all of your debts, such as your mortgage, car loan and credit card balances, from your total assets. The result is your net worth.

Recalculate your net worth each month as you pay your bills and put money into your emergency savings and retirement accounts. Watching that number first become less negative and then grow positively at such a rapid pace is motivating and will inspire you to stay on track.

Think Differently

One of the joys and challenges to living the savvy life is that you will start to think differently than the people around you. We encourage it! You don't have to live the way everyone else does. You should live the way that will make you happiest. Take a few steps back from each situation and look at it from your savvy perspective. It's possible you will see solutions to situations that won't occur to others.

In the FFIT@home program (www.FFIT.tv) Coach Erika and I created, we encourage our members to be FFIT Rebels. Sadly, although more and more focus is put on losing weight with a new diet craze launched every month, obesity has reached epidemic proportions. What "everyone" is doing isn't working. Restaurant portion sizes are out of control. It seems that each new diet conflicts with the message of the previous diet which causes confusion and frustration.

To an extent, living the savvy life is like being a Financial Rebel. You don't have to buy what everyone is buying, drive what everyone is driving, vacation where everyone is vacationing, or live where everyone is living. You are the designer of your life.

You will find occasionally that people will resist the choices you are making. In many instances, it makes them uncomfortable, because they don't have the same drive to obtain what they truly want.

I personally experienced a difficult situation involving this type of social pressure. When Paul and I started talking about remodeling our house we decided to begin cutting back our spending so we could pay for as much of the remodel as possible out of pocket.

Shortly after making this decision, a friend called to see if I wanted to go out to dinner with her. I explained why Paul and I were cutting back our expenses and that I would be happy to go out with her, but that I would just have coffee. It was a very unpleasant experience. During dinner she kept talking about the fact that I was only having coffee. It got to the point that she was almost making fun of me. I kept my composure and endured the evening. Even after dinner, she continued to bring it up.

It was a very difficult decision, but I knew the relationship was no longer going to work for me. If she couldn't understand my reasons for wanting to curb my spending, the friendship wasn't going to last. To this day, I am still very sad about the loss of the friendship. At the same time, I am proud of myself for standing by my decision to do what I needed to do for myself and my family. Social pressure can be very powerful and it can be difficult to rebel against. You just have to decide who is going to spend your money - you, or your friends?

You are the designer of your life. You decide what is important to you. You define your personal style. You are empowered and have the ability to achieve your goals. Put into action the plan you created in Chapter 12 and work toward it one step at a time.

You Can Count on *The Savvy Life*

It is our job as the publishers of *The Savvy Life* (TheSavvyLife.com) to keep you motivated. Through our articles and weekly newsletter we strive to keep you inspired and excited about your savvy lifestyle.

The Savvy Life is continuously updated and offers many free tools. We publish original articles on:

- Home
- Entertainment
- Wardrobe
- Beauty
- Food
- Money

We scour articles from around the world that relate to your savvy lifestyle and post them in the World Report section. I also post a personal blog about my own adventures of living *The Savvy Life*.

Our weekly email newsletter offers money saving tips and information on the latest news from the website. Let *The Savvy Life* be an additional tool to help you create the life you want.

Chapter 17

Your Savvy Life

As we told you at the beginning of this book, we want you to gain control of your finances and focus your spending on what you truly want. We want you to stop worrying about your credit card bills or how you're going to make it to the next pay period. Life is a wonderful adventure and money should be a tool, not an obstacle to living it to the fullest.

Remember that *Living the Savvy Life* isn't just about money. It's about turning your home into a sanctuary. It's about taking pleasure in every moment of your time off. It's about building a wardrobe and beauty routine that make you feel gorgeous. It's about nourishing your body and soul with delicious food.

You are the artist and a savvy life is yours to create.

• • • • • • • • •

One of the greatest gifts my parents gave me was the knowledge that I could achieve anything I set my mind to. In turn, I am passing that gift on to you.

Go forth! The Savvy Life awaits you!

Chapter 18

Favorite Resources

In addition to the many resources mentioned throughout this book, we have compiled a list of some additional favorites for each of the areas of your life; home, entertainment, wardrobe, beauty, food and money.

Home

Sink Reflections, **by Marla Cilley - The Flylady**
The Flylady shows you how to fly out of CHAOS (Can't Have Anyone Over Syndrome) and turn your home into a sanctuary.

Frugal Luxuries, **by Tracey McBride**
A thoroughly enjoyable read filled with simple and affordable pleasures to enhance your life.

Joie de Vivre: Simple French Style for Every Day Living, **by Robert Arbor**
A French primer on learning to enjoy the every day details of life.

Home Comforts: The Art and Science of Keeping House,
by Cheryl Mendelson
An easy to read "encyclopedia" of keeping house. This book also makes a great gift for a new home owner.

Martha Stewart

Martha Stewart made home keeping cool again. Her books, magazine and television show offer inspiration for resourceful and creative nesting.

BeJane.com

An online community to help women who are looking to do home improvement projects but don't know where to get started.

Entertainment

Frugal Luxuries by the Seasons: Celebrate the Holidays with Elegance and Simplicity – on Any Income, **By Tracey McBride**

A beautifully written guide to show you how to enrich your holidays and enjoy the rhythm of the seasons.

The New York Times - **Budget Travel Section**

A budget travel guide from *The New York Times* with tips and recommendations that won't break the bank

Rachael Ray Show & *Every Day with Rachael Ray*

Both resources offer fun, easy and affordable entertaining ideas.

Play It Again Sports

Neighborhood sporting goods stores that buy, sell and trade quality used sports equipment.

Entertainment.com

The publisher of *The Entertainment Book*, where you can save with their restaurant coupons, discounts on shopping, attractions, travel and much more.

BoardGameGeek.com

One of Paul's favorite sites for researching board games.

Wardrobe

Tim Gunn: A Guide to Quality, Taste and Style, **by Tim Gunn with Kate Moloney**
Fashion wisdom from the well respected mentor of Project Runway.

Frumpy to Foxy in 15 Minutes Flat, **by Elycia Rubin and Rita Mauceri**
Quick, easy tips that transform you (like the title says) from frumpy to foxy.

What Not to Wear, **TLC Channel**
Get fashion tips and tricks on *What Not to Wear* with Stacy London and Clinton Kelly.

TheBudgetFashionista.net
Find out about the latest styles, secret celebrity fashion tips and discount designer fashions.

TheRecessionista.com
The Recessionista blog strives to help you remain fashionable on a minimal budget.

TheBudgetBabe.com
Fashion, beauty and style on a budget including designer and celebrity looks for less.

Beauty

Rite Aid
Rite Aid's cosmetics return policy ensures you don't waste money on makeup that isn't right for you.

Sephora
Sephora stores and website offers one of the most extensive collections of skin care, cosmetics, fragrance and hair products.

The Five Minute Face, by Carmindy
The kind-hearted makeup artist from *What Not to Wear* shows you how to use the right products in the right places to enhance your own unique, natural beauty.

Frederic Fekkai: A Year of Style, by Fredric Fekkai
An inspiring month-by-month guide to simple beauty. The book itself is beautiful and something to read for pleasure as well as for information.

Allure Magazine
Allure's Best of Beauty list is the equivalent of the *Good Housekeeping* seal of approval, but for beauty products.

InStyle
A fun to read resource on the latest fashion and beauty. *InStyle* also features both high end and affordable products.

Food

Betty Crocker Cookbooks
Every house should own at least one basic cookbook. *The Betty Crocker* cookbook my grandmother gave me when I turned 21 is one of my greatest, well used treasures.

Chef2Chef.net
Beginner and advanced home chefs can learn from this addictive and expansive cooking site.

SavingDinner.com
Leanne Ely's site encourages families to get back to sharing meals together by offering recipes, menu planning and grocery shopping lists.

FoodTV & FoodTV.com
The Food Network is devoted to sharing recipes, video demonstrations, cooking techniques, quick and easy meals, healthy eating and more.

Epicurious.com
The website is filled with over 20,000 recipes from *Gourmet* and *Bon Appétit* magazines.

AllRecipes.com
An online recipe exchange community with over 40,000 free recipes plus helpful reviews.

Money

Living Rich by Spending Smart, **by Gregory Karp**
Award-winning personal finance columnist Gregory Karp shows you the fastest and easiest way to eliminate debt, achieve financial security and get rich by controlling your spending.

The Automatic Millionaire, **by David Bach**
A powerful one-step plan to help you live and finish rich.

The Millionaire Next Door, **by Thomas J. Stanley and William D. Danko**
The surprising secrets of America's wealthy. This is an eye opening book helping you realize wealth is more attainable than you may think.

Women & Money, **by Suze Orman**
Suze wants you and every woman you know to take control of your lives by taking control of your finances.

Kiplinger Magazine & **Kiplinger.com**
Easy to read and understand personal finance advice.

Bankrate.com
A rich source of up-to-date financial information including personal finance calculators.

About the Authors

Melissa Tosetti

Melissa Tosetti is the founder of the online magazine, *The Savvy Life*. She is an author, speaker and teacher. Melissa's passion is to show Americans how step off the pendulum that swings from overspending to extreme frugality. She believes balance is the key to enjoying life with financial security.

Melissa co-wrote a chapter on savvy living for the book, *Your Military Family Network*. She has appeared on numerous episodes of *Pocket the Difference* on the Fine Living Network, *The Real Deal with Jeanette Pavini* and on *Eye on the Bay*. She is repeatedly quoted in nationwide publications including *U.S. News & World Report*, *TodayShow. com*, *Chicago Tribune* and *Detroit News*. She has chaired panels on savvy living at the Professional Businesswomen of California conferences in San Francisco and Sacramento. She also teaches courses on savvy living at Chabot College in Hayward, CA and around the San Francisco Bay Area.

Melissa is a second degree black belt in Choy Lay Fut Kung Fu and moonlights at Fearless Fitness in Foster City, CA. She teaches Kung Fu and fitness classes. In addition to teaching at Fearless, she is also a coach for FFIT@home (www.FFIT.tv), which allows you to download Fearless Fitness' Intensity Training classes to do in the privacy of your own home as well as offering nutrition advice and support.

Whether talking about money or calories and fitness, Melissa's message is still the same - balance.

Melissa loves adventuring with her husband Paul and son Dante whether it is in their own backyard or while traveling across the world. In her downtime, Melissa can be found cooking, gardening, horseback riding, reading, or watching the Food Network and the History Channel.

Melissa can be reached at:
(650) 299-1500
Melissa@TheSavvyLife.com
Twitter.com/TheSavvyLife
Facebook.com/The Savvy Life

Kevin Gibbons

Kevin Gibbons is the Managing Editor of *The Savvy Life*. Kevin brings his 20 years' experience as an engineer and program manager in the high-tech arena to help keep *The Savvy Life* running smoothly. In addition to maintaining production schedules, working with Melissa to determine content and editing, Kevin also contributes articles on managing finances and cooking.

Kevin also co-wrote a chapter on savvy living for the book, *Your Military Family Network*.

A scientist by training, Kevin lives the savvy life as it allows him to afford his assorted hobbies which range from photography to motorcycle riding to miniatures modeling to gourmet cooking to compulsively reading everything he can find. Kevin and his wife live in the San Francisco Bay Area. Their house is full of 19th century and Art Deco antiques they found at below-market prices and bought by saving and purchasing on layaway.

Kevin can be reached at:
(650) 299-1500
Kevin@TheSavvyLife.com
FaceBook.com/The Savvy Life

BUY A SHARE OF THE FUTURE IN YOUR COMMUNITY

These certificates make great holiday, graduation and birthday gifts that can be personalized with the recipient's name. The cost of one S.H.A.R.E. or one square foot is $54.17. The personalized certificate is suitable for framing and will state the number of shares purchased and the amount of each share, as well as the recipient's name. The home that you participate in "building" will last for many years and will continue to grow in value.

Here is a sample SHARE certificate:

THIS CERTIFIES THAT

YOUR NAME HERE

HAS INVESTED IN A HOME FOR A DESERVING FAMILY

1985-2005

TWENTY YEARS OF BUILDING FUTURES IN OUR COMMUNITY ONE HOME AT A TIME

1200 SQUARE FOOT HOUSE @ $65,000 = $54.17 PER SQUARE FOOT
This certificate represents a tax deductible donation. It has no cash value.

YES, I WOULD LIKE TO HELP!

I support the work that Habitat for Humanity does and I want to be part of the excitement! As a donor, I will receive periodic updates on your construction activities but, more importantly, I know my gift will help a family in our community realize the dream of homeownership. **I would like to SHARE in your efforts against substandard housing in my community!** *(Please print below)*

PLEASE SEND ME _____ SHARES at $54.17 EACH = $ $_____

In Honor Of: _____

Occasion: (Circle One)   HOLIDAY   BIRTHDAY   ANNIVERSARY

OTHER: _____

Address of Recipient: _____

Gift From: _____ *Donor Address:* _____

Donor Email: _____

I AM ENCLOSING A CHECK FOR $ $_____ PAYABLE TO HABITAT FOR HUMANITY <u>OR</u> PLEASE CHARGE MY VISA OR MASTERCARD *(CIRCLE ONE)*

Card Number _____ Expiration Date: _____

Name as it appears on Credit Card _____ Charge Amount $ _____

Signature _____

Billing Address _____

Telephone # Day _____ Eve _____

PLEASE NOTE: Your contribution is tax-deductible to the fullest extent allowed by law.
Habitat for Humanity • P.O. Box 1443 • Newport News, VA 23601 • 757-596-5553
www.HelpHabitatforHumanity.org

CPSIA information can be obtained at www.ICGtesting.com
Printed in the USA
LVOW101447170212

269203LV00001B/1/P